50 Italian Pasta Recipes for Home

By: Kelly Johnson

Table of Contents

- Spaghetti Carbonara
- Fettuccine Alfredo
- Linguine with Clam Sauce
- Penne all'Arrabbiata
- Lasagna Bolognese
- Pasta Primavera
- Gnocchi alla Sorrentina
- Ravioli with Sage Butter Sauce
- Rigatoni with Sausage and Peppers
- Cacio e Pepe
- Spaghetti Aglio e Olio
- Tagliatelle with Mushroom Cream Sauce
- Orecchiette with Broccoli Rabe and Sausage
- Pappardelle with Wild Boar Ragu
- Cannelloni with Spinach and Ricotta
- Bucatini all'Amatriciana
- Tortellini in Brodo
- Farfalle with Pesto Genovese
- Cavatelli with Tomato and Basil
- Paccheri with Eggplant and Mozzarella
- Trofie al Pesto
- Stuffed Shells with Ricotta and Spinach
- Spaghetti Puttanesca
- Pappardelle with Duck Ragout
- Fettuccine with Shrimp Scampi
- Lasagna al Forno
- Linguine with Lobster
- Penne alla Vodka
- Ravioli di Zucca (Pumpkin Ravioli)
- Tagliatelle with Bolognese Sauce
- Orecchiette with Broccoli and Anchovies
- Spaghetti alle Vongole
- Tortellini alla Panna
- Farfalle with Chicken and Sun-Dried Tomatoes
- Cavatappi with Four Cheese Sauce

- Garganelli with Asparagus and Pancetta
- Rigatoni with Eggplant and Tomato Sauce
- Cannelloni al Forno
- Fusilli with Roasted Vegetables
- Pappardelle with Porcini Mushrooms
- Lasagna Roll-Ups
- Linguine with Lemon and Garlic Shrimp
- Penne with Arrabbiata Sauce
- Ravioli with Spinach and Ricotta
- Spaghetti alla Puttanesca
- Tagliatelle with Creamy Mushroom Sauce
- Orecchiette with Sausage and Broccoli Rabe
- Farfalle with Salmon and Cream Sauce
- Cavatelli with Rapini and Sausage
- Rigatoni with Cherry Tomato Sauce and Burrata

Spaghetti Carbonara

Ingredients:

- 12 ounces (340g) spaghetti
- 4 large eggs
- 1 cup (100g) grated Parmesan cheese, plus extra for serving
- 8 slices of pancetta or bacon, diced
- 3 cloves garlic, minced
- 1/4 cup (60ml) dry white wine (optional)
- Salt and black pepper to taste
- Fresh parsley, chopped (for garnish)

Instructions:

1. Cook the Spaghetti:

    Bring a large pot of salted water to a boil.
    Add the spaghetti and cook according to the package instructions until al dente.
    Reserve 1 cup of pasta cooking water, then drain the spaghetti.

2. Prepare the Sauce:

    In a mixing bowl, whisk together the eggs and grated Parmesan cheese until well combined. Set aside.

3. Cook the Pancetta/Bacon:

    In a large skillet, cook the diced pancetta or bacon over medium heat until crispy and golden brown, about 5-7 minutes.
    Add the minced garlic to the skillet and cook for an additional 1-2 minutes until fragrant.

4. Combine the Pasta and Sauce:

    If using, pour the white wine into the skillet and cook for 1-2 minutes, scraping up any browned bits from the bottom of the pan.
    Reduce the heat to low and add the cooked spaghetti to the skillet, tossing to coat it in the pancetta/bacon and garlic mixture.

5. Add the Egg Mixture:

Remove the skillet from the heat.
Pour the egg and Parmesan mixture over the hot spaghetti, tossing quickly and continuously to coat the pasta evenly. The residual heat will cook the eggs and create a creamy sauce.
If the sauce seems too thick, add a splash of reserved pasta cooking water to loosen it up.

6. Season and Serve:

Season the Spaghetti Carbonara with salt and black pepper to taste.
Garnish with chopped fresh parsley and extra grated Parmesan cheese, if desired.
Serve immediately, piping hot, and enjoy!

Spaghetti Carbonara is best enjoyed fresh and hot, so serve it right away for the best taste and texture.

Fettuccine Alfredo

Ingredients:

- 12 ounces (340g) fettuccine pasta
- 1/2 cup (1 stick) unsalted butter
- 1 cup heavy cream
- 1 1/2 cups grated Parmesan cheese
- Salt and freshly ground black pepper to taste
- Fresh parsley, chopped (for garnish)
- Optional: Additional grated Parmesan cheese for serving

Instructions:

1. Cook the Pasta:

    Bring a large pot of salted water to a boil.
    Add the fettuccine pasta and cook according to the package instructions until al dente.
    Reserve 1 cup of pasta cooking water, then drain the pasta and set aside.

2. Prepare the Sauce:

    In a large skillet or saucepan, melt the unsalted butter over medium heat.
    Once the butter is melted, pour in the heavy cream and bring it to a simmer. Cook for 2-3 minutes, stirring occasionally.
    Reduce the heat to low and gradually add the grated Parmesan cheese to the skillet, stirring constantly until the cheese is melted and the sauce is smooth and creamy.
    If the sauce is too thick, gradually add a splash of reserved pasta cooking water until you reach your desired consistency.

3. Combine the Pasta and Sauce:

    Add the cooked fettuccine pasta to the skillet with the Alfredo sauce, tossing to coat the pasta evenly.
    Season the Fettuccine Alfredo with salt and freshly ground black pepper to taste. Be cautious with the salt as Parmesan cheese is salty.
    Continue to cook the pasta in the sauce for another minute or two until heated through.

4. Serve:

    Transfer the Fettuccine Alfredo to serving plates or a large serving dish.
    Garnish with chopped fresh parsley and additional grated Parmesan cheese if desired.
    Serve immediately, piping hot, and enjoy!

Fettuccine Alfredo is a comforting and indulgent dish that is best enjoyed fresh and hot. Serve it as a main course or alongside your favorite protein for a delicious meal.

Linguine with Clam Sauce

Ingredients:

- 12 ounces (340g) linguine pasta
- 2 tablespoons olive oil
- 4 cloves garlic, minced
- 1/4 teaspoon red pepper flakes (adjust to taste)
- 2 cans (6.5 ounces each) chopped clams, drained, juice reserved
- 1/2 cup dry white wine
- 1/2 cup clam juice (reserved from canned clams or store-bought)
- 1/4 cup fresh parsley, chopped
- Salt and freshly ground black pepper to taste
- Grated Parmesan cheese for serving (optional)

Instructions:

1. Cook the Pasta:

    Bring a large pot of salted water to a boil.
    Add the linguine pasta and cook according to the package instructions until al dente.
    Reserve 1 cup of pasta cooking water, then drain the pasta and set aside.

2. Prepare the Clam Sauce:

    In a large skillet, heat the olive oil over medium heat.
    Add the minced garlic and red pepper flakes to the skillet and sauté for 1-2 minutes until fragrant.
    Add the chopped clams to the skillet and sauté for another 1-2 minutes.
    Pour in the dry white wine and clam juice, scraping up any browned bits from the bottom of the skillet.
    Bring the mixture to a simmer and cook for 3-4 minutes to allow the flavors to meld together.

3. Combine the Pasta and Sauce:

    Add the cooked linguine pasta to the skillet with the clam sauce, tossing to coat the pasta evenly.
    If the sauce seems too thick, gradually add a splash of reserved pasta cooking water until you reach your desired consistency.
    Stir in the chopped fresh parsley and season the Linguine with Clam Sauce with salt and freshly ground black pepper to taste.

4. Serve:

> Transfer the Linguine with Clam Sauce to serving plates or a large serving dish.
> Optionally, sprinkle grated Parmesan cheese over the top for added flavor.
> Serve immediately, piping hot, and enjoy!

Linguine with Clam Sauce is a delicious and comforting pasta dish that is perfect for seafood lovers. Serve it as a main course for a satisfying meal.

Penne all'Arrabbiata

Ingredients:

- 12 ounces (340g) penne pasta
- 2 tablespoons olive oil
- 4 cloves garlic, minced
- 1/2 teaspoon red pepper flakes (adjust to taste)
- 1 can (14.5 ounces) diced tomatoes
- 2 tablespoons tomato paste
- 1/4 cup fresh parsley, chopped
- Salt to taste
- Grated Parmesan cheese for serving (optional)

Instructions:

1. Cook the Pasta:

   Bring a large pot of salted water to a boil.
   Add the penne pasta and cook according to the package instructions until al dente.
   Reserve 1 cup of pasta cooking water, then drain the pasta and set aside.

2. Prepare the Arrabbiata Sauce:

   In a large skillet, heat the olive oil over medium heat.
   Add the minced garlic and red pepper flakes to the skillet and sauté for 1-2 minutes until fragrant.
   Add the diced tomatoes (with their juices) and tomato paste to the skillet, stirring to combine.
   Bring the sauce to a simmer and cook for 8-10 minutes, stirring occasionally, until the flavors meld together and the sauce thickens slightly.

3. Combine the Pasta and Sauce:

   Add the cooked penne pasta to the skillet with the Arrabbiata sauce, tossing to coat the pasta evenly.
   If the sauce seems too thick, gradually add a splash of reserved pasta cooking water until you reach your desired consistency.
   Stir in the chopped fresh parsley and season the Penne all'Arrabbiata with salt to taste.

4. Serve:

   Transfer the Penne all'Arrabbiata to serving plates or a large serving dish.

Optionally, sprinkle grated Parmesan cheese over the top for added flavor.
Serve immediately, piping hot, and enjoy!

Penne all'Arrabbiata is a classic Italian pasta dish known for its spicy tomato sauce. It's quick and easy to make, yet bursting with flavor. Serve it as a main course for a satisfying and delicious meal.

Lasagna Bolognese

Ingredients:

For the Bolognese Sauce:

- 1 tablespoon olive oil
- 1 onion, finely chopped
- 2 carrots, finely chopped
- 2 celery stalks, finely chopped
- 4 cloves garlic, minced
- 1 pound (450g) ground beef
- 1 pound (450g) ground pork
- 1 can (14.5 ounces) crushed tomatoes
- 1/2 cup beef or chicken broth
- 1/2 cup red wine (optional)
- 2 tablespoons tomato paste
- 1 teaspoon dried oregano
- 1 teaspoon dried basil
- Salt and pepper to taste

For the Lasagna:

- 9 lasagna noodles, cooked according to package instructions
- 3 cups shredded mozzarella cheese
- 1 cup grated Parmesan cheese
- Fresh basil leaves for garnish (optional)

Instructions:

1. Prepare the Bolognese Sauce:

   Heat olive oil in a large skillet or Dutch oven over medium heat.
   Add the chopped onion, carrots, and celery to the skillet. Cook, stirring occasionally, until the vegetables are softened, about 5-7 minutes.
   Add the minced garlic and cook for an additional minute until fragrant.
   Add the ground beef and ground pork to the skillet. Cook, breaking up the meat with a spoon, until browned and cooked through.
   Stir in the crushed tomatoes, beef or chicken broth, red wine (if using), tomato paste, dried oregano, and dried basil. Season with salt and pepper to taste.
   Bring the sauce to a simmer, then reduce the heat to low and let it simmer gently for about 30-40 minutes, stirring occasionally, until thickened.

2. Assemble the Lasagna:

> Preheat the oven to 375°F (190°C).
> Spread a thin layer of Bolognese sauce on the bottom of a 9x13-inch baking dish.
> Place a layer of cooked lasagna noodles on top of the sauce, slightly overlapping them.
> Spread a layer of Bolognese sauce over the noodles, then sprinkle with shredded mozzarella cheese and grated Parmesan cheese.
> Repeat the layers, ending with a layer of sauce and cheese on top.

3. Bake the Lasagna:

> Cover the baking dish with aluminum foil and bake in the preheated oven for 25 minutes.
> Remove the foil and bake for an additional 10-15 minutes, or until the cheese is melted and bubbly, and the edges are golden brown.
> Remove the lasagna from the oven and let it rest for 10 minutes before slicing.
> Garnish with fresh basil leaves if desired.
> Serve hot and enjoy your delicious Lasagna Bolognese!

This Lasagna Bolognese is rich, hearty, and full of flavor, making it a perfect comfort food dish for family gatherings or special occasions.

Pasta Primavera

Ingredients:

- 12 ounces (340g) fettuccine or spaghetti
- 2 tablespoons olive oil
- 4 cloves garlic, minced
- 1 small onion, thinly sliced
- 2 carrots, julienned
- 1 small zucchini, julienned
- 1 small yellow squash, julienned
- 1 cup cherry tomatoes, halved
- 1 cup broccoli florets
- 1 cup bell peppers, thinly sliced (assorted colors)
- 1/2 cup peas (fresh or frozen)
- 1/2 cup vegetable broth or chicken broth
- 1/4 cup heavy cream or half-and-half (optional)
- 1/4 cup grated Parmesan cheese
- Salt and pepper to taste
- Fresh basil leaves, chopped, for garnish

Instructions:

1. Cook the Pasta:

    Bring a large pot of salted water to a boil.
    Add the pasta and cook according to the package instructions until al dente.
    Reserve 1 cup of pasta cooking water, then drain the pasta and set aside.

2. Prepare the Vegetables:

    In a large skillet or sauté pan, heat the olive oil over medium heat.
    Add the minced garlic and sliced onion to the skillet. Cook for 2-3 minutes until softened and fragrant.
    Add the julienned carrots, zucchini, yellow squash, cherry tomatoes, broccoli florets, bell peppers, and peas to the skillet. Cook, stirring occasionally, for 5-7 minutes until the vegetables are tender-crisp.

3. Make the Sauce:

Pour the vegetable or chicken broth into the skillet with the cooked vegetables. Stir to combine.
   If using, add the heavy cream or half-and-half to the skillet, stirring until heated through.
   Season the sauce with salt and pepper to taste.

4. Combine the Pasta and Vegetables:

   Add the cooked pasta to the skillet with the vegetable sauce, tossing to coat the pasta evenly.
   If the sauce seems too thick, gradually add a splash of reserved pasta cooking water until you reach your desired consistency.

5. Finish and Serve:

   Sprinkle grated Parmesan cheese over the Pasta Primavera and toss to combine.
   Garnish with chopped fresh basil leaves for added flavor and freshness.
   Serve immediately, piping hot, and enjoy!

Pasta Primavera is a delicious and vibrant dish that celebrates the flavors of spring and summer. It's versatile and adaptable, so feel free to customize it with your favorite vegetables and herbs.

Gnocchi alla Sorrentina

Ingredients:

- 1 pound (450g) potato gnocchi
- 2 cups marinara sauce or tomato passata
- 8 ounces (225g) fresh mozzarella, sliced
- 1/4 cup grated Parmesan cheese
- Fresh basil leaves, torn
- Salt and pepper to taste
- Olive oil for drizzling

Instructions:

1. Preheat the Oven:

    Preheat your oven to 375°F (190°C).

2. Cook the Gnocchi:

    Bring a large pot of salted water to a boil.
    Cook the potato gnocchi according to the package instructions until they float to the surface, indicating they're cooked. Drain well.

3. Assemble the Dish:

    In a baking dish, spread a thin layer of marinara sauce or tomato passata.
    Arrange the cooked gnocchi in the baking dish.
    Pour the remaining marinara sauce or passata over the gnocchi, ensuring they are well coated.
    Top the gnocchi with slices of fresh mozzarella cheese.
    Sprinkle grated Parmesan cheese over the top.
    Season with salt and pepper to taste.
    Scatter torn fresh basil leaves over the dish.

4. Bake:

    Transfer the baking dish to the preheated oven.
    Bake for about 20-25 minutes, or until the cheese is melted and bubbly and the edges are golden brown.

5. Serve:

Once baked, remove the Gnocchi alla Sorrentina from the oven.
Drizzle with a little olive oil.
Garnish with additional torn basil leaves, if desired.
Serve hot and enjoy!

Gnocchi alla Sorrentina is a comforting and flavorful dish that's perfect for a cozy dinner. The combination of pillowy gnocchi, rich tomato sauce, gooey mozzarella, and fragrant basil creates a truly satisfying meal.

Ravioli with Sage Butter Sauce

Ingredients:

- 1 pound (450g) store-bought or homemade ravioli (your choice of filling)
- 1/2 cup (1 stick) unsalted butter
- 8-10 fresh sage leaves
- 1/4 cup grated Parmesan cheese, plus extra for serving
- Salt and freshly ground black pepper to taste

Instructions:

1. Cook the Ravioli:

    Bring a large pot of salted water to a boil.
    Add the ravioli to the boiling water and cook according to the package instructions (if store-bought) or until they float to the surface (if homemade). This usually takes about 3-4 minutes for fresh ravioli or 8-10 minutes for frozen.
    Once cooked, remove the ravioli from the water using a slotted spoon and transfer them to a serving dish.

2. Make the Sage Butter Sauce:

    In a large skillet, melt the unsalted butter over medium heat.
    Add the fresh sage leaves to the skillet and cook for 1-2 minutes, or until they become fragrant and crispy. Be careful not to burn them.
    Remove the sage leaves from the skillet and set them aside.
    Continue to cook the butter until it turns a light golden brown color, about 2-3 minutes, while stirring frequently.
    Remove the skillet from the heat and let it cool slightly.

3. Toss the Ravioli:

    Pour the sage butter sauce over the cooked ravioli in the serving dish.
    Gently toss the ravioli in the sauce until they are evenly coated.

4. Serve:

    Sprinkle grated Parmesan cheese over the top of the ravioli.
    Season with salt and freshly ground black pepper to taste.
    Garnish with the crispy sage leaves.

Serve immediately, piping hot, with extra Parmesan cheese on the side for serving.

Ravioli with sage butter sauce is a delightful dish that's perfect for a special occasion or a cozy weeknight dinner. The combination of tender pasta, rich buttery sauce, and aromatic sage creates a harmonious and comforting meal. Enjoy!

Rigatoni with Sausage and Peppers

Ingredients:

- 12 ounces (340g) rigatoni pasta
- 1 pound (450g) Italian sausage (sweet or spicy), casings removed
- 2 bell peppers (red, yellow, or green), thinly sliced
- 1 onion, thinly sliced
- 3 cloves garlic, minced
- 1 can (14.5 ounces) diced tomatoes
- 1/2 cup tomato sauce
- 1 teaspoon dried oregano
- 1 teaspoon dried basil
- Salt and freshly ground black pepper to taste
- Grated Parmesan cheese for serving
- Fresh basil leaves for garnish (optional)

Instructions:

1. Cook the Rigatoni:

    Bring a large pot of salted water to a boil.
    Add the rigatoni pasta and cook according to the package instructions until al dente.
    Reserve 1 cup of pasta cooking water, then drain the pasta and set aside.

2. Cook the Sausage and Peppers:

    In a large skillet or sauté pan, cook the Italian sausage over medium heat, breaking it up with a spoon, until browned and cooked through.
    Remove the cooked sausage from the skillet and set it aside.
    In the same skillet, add the sliced bell peppers and onion. Cook until they are softened and slightly caramelized, about 5-7 minutes.
    Add the minced garlic to the skillet and cook for an additional minute until fragrant.

3. Make the Sauce:

    Return the cooked sausage to the skillet with the peppers and onions.
    Stir in the diced tomatoes, tomato sauce, dried oregano, and dried basil.
    Season with salt and freshly ground black pepper to taste.

Let the sauce simmer for 10-15 minutes to allow the flavors to meld together.

4. Combine the Pasta and Sauce:

    Add the cooked rigatoni pasta to the skillet with the sausage and peppers. Toss everything together until the pasta is well coated in the sauce. If the sauce seems too thick, add a splash of reserved pasta cooking water to loosen it up.

5. Serve:

    Transfer the Rigatoni with Sausage and Peppers to serving plates or a large serving dish.
    Garnish with grated Parmesan cheese and fresh basil leaves, if desired.
    Serve hot and enjoy!

Rigatoni with sausage and peppers is a comforting and satisfying dish that's sure to please your taste buds. It's perfect for a family dinner or entertaining guests. Enjoy!

Cacio e Pepe

Ingredients:

- 12 ounces (340g) spaghetti or tonnarelli pasta
- 1 1/2 cups finely grated Pecorino Romano cheese
- 1 teaspoon freshly ground black pepper
- Salt for pasta water

Instructions:

1. Cook the Pasta:

    Bring a large pot of salted water to a boil.
    Add the spaghetti or tonnarelli pasta and cook according to the package instructions until al dente. Reserve about 1 cup of pasta cooking water, then drain the pasta and set aside.

2. Toast the Black Pepper:

    While the pasta is cooking, heat a large skillet over medium heat.
    Add the freshly ground black pepper to the skillet and toast it for about 1 minute, stirring constantly, until fragrant. Be careful not to burn it.

3. Make the Sauce:

    Once the pasta is cooked and drained, return the skillet with the toasted black pepper to low heat.
    Add about 3/4 cup of the reserved pasta cooking water to the skillet and bring it to a simmer.
    Gradually whisk in the finely grated Pecorino Romano cheese, stirring constantly, until the cheese has melted and the sauce is smooth and creamy. It's important to do this gradually to prevent clumping.
    If the sauce seems too thick, add more pasta cooking water as needed until you reach your desired consistency.

4. Combine the Pasta and Sauce:

    Add the cooked spaghetti or tonnarelli pasta to the skillet with the sauce.
    Toss everything together gently until the pasta is well coated in the sauce.
    If the sauce becomes too thick, you can add a little more pasta cooking water to loosen it up.

5. Serve:

    Transfer the Cacio e Pepe to serving plates or bowls.
    Sprinkle with an extra dusting of freshly ground black pepper and finely grated Pecorino Romano cheese on top.
    Serve immediately while piping hot and enjoy!

Cacio e Pepe is best served immediately after making it to enjoy the creamy texture of the sauce. It's a simple yet incredibly flavorful dish that celebrates the beauty of high-quality ingredients like Pecorino Romano cheese and black pepper.

Spaghetti Aglio e Olio

Ingredients:

- 12 ounces (340g) spaghetti
- 1/2 cup extra virgin olive oil
- 6 cloves garlic, thinly sliced
- 1 teaspoon red pepper flakes (adjust to taste)
- 1/4 cup chopped fresh parsley
- Salt for pasta water
- Grated Parmesan cheese for serving (optional)

Instructions:

1. Cook the Spaghetti:

   Bring a large pot of salted water to a boil.
   Add the spaghetti and cook according to the package instructions until al dente.
   Reserve 1 cup of pasta cooking water, then drain the spaghetti and set it aside.

2. Prepare the Sauce:

   While the pasta is cooking, heat the extra virgin olive oil in a large skillet over medium heat.
   Add the thinly sliced garlic to the skillet and cook for 2-3 minutes, or until it becomes golden brown and fragrant. Be careful not to burn the garlic.
   Add the red pepper flakes to the skillet and cook for an additional 1-2 minutes, stirring constantly.
   Remove the skillet from the heat and set it aside.

3. Combine the Spaghetti and Sauce:

   Once the spaghetti is cooked and drained, add it to the skillet with the garlic and red pepper flakes.
   Toss the spaghetti in the olive oil mixture until it is well coated.
   If the spaghetti seems dry, you can add some of the reserved pasta cooking water to loosen it up.
   Stir in the chopped fresh parsley and toss to combine.

4. Serve:

   Transfer the Spaghetti Aglio e Olio to serving plates or bowls.
   Optionally, sprinkle with grated Parmesan cheese for extra flavor.

Serve immediately while piping hot and enjoy!

Spaghetti Aglio e Olio is a simple yet incredibly flavorful dish that highlights the beauty of high-quality ingredients like olive oil, garlic, and red pepper flakes. It's perfect for a quick and satisfying meal any day of the week.

Tagliatelle with Mushroom Cream Sauce

Ingredients:

- 12 ounces (340g) tagliatelle pasta
- 2 tablespoons unsalted butter
- 2 tablespoons olive oil
- 1 pound (450g) mixed mushrooms (such as cremini, shiitake, and oyster), sliced
- 3 cloves garlic, minced
- 1/2 cup dry white wine (optional)
- 1 cup heavy cream
- 1/2 cup grated Parmesan cheese, plus extra for serving
- Salt and freshly ground black pepper to taste
- Chopped fresh parsley for garnish (optional)

Instructions:

1. Cook the Tagliatelle:

    Bring a large pot of salted water to a boil.
    Add the tagliatelle pasta and cook according to the package instructions until al dente.
    Reserve 1 cup of pasta cooking water, then drain the pasta and set it aside.

2. Sauté the Mushrooms:

    In a large skillet or sauté pan, melt the butter with the olive oil over medium heat.
    Add the sliced mushrooms to the skillet and cook, stirring occasionally, until they are golden brown and tender, about 8-10 minutes.
    Add the minced garlic to the skillet and cook for an additional 1-2 minutes until fragrant.
    If using, pour in the dry white wine and cook for 2-3 minutes until the alcohol evaporates.

3. Make the Cream Sauce:

    Reduce the heat to low and pour the heavy cream into the skillet with the mushrooms.
    Stir in the grated Parmesan cheese until it is melted and the sauce is smooth and creamy.
    Season with salt and freshly ground black pepper to taste.

4. Combine the Pasta and Sauce:

 Add the cooked tagliatelle pasta to the skillet with the mushroom cream sauce. Toss everything together gently until the pasta is well coated in the sauce. If the sauce seems too thick, you can add a splash of reserved pasta cooking water to loosen it up.

5. Serve:

 Transfer the Tagliatelle with Mushroom Cream Sauce to serving plates or bowls. Optionally, sprinkle with extra grated Parmesan cheese and chopped fresh parsley for garnish.
 Serve immediately, piping hot, and enjoy!

Tagliatelle with mushroom cream sauce is a luxurious and comforting dish that's perfect for a cozy dinner at home. The combination of earthy mushrooms, creamy sauce, and tender pasta creates a satisfying meal that will impress your family and friends.

Orecchiette with Broccoli Rabe and Sausage

Ingredients:

- 12 ounces (340g) orecchiette pasta
- 1 pound (450g) sweet or hot Italian sausage, casings removed
- 1 bunch broccoli rabe, trimmed and chopped into bite-sized pieces
- 4 cloves garlic, minced
- 1/2 teaspoon red pepper flakes (adjust to taste)
- 1/4 cup extra virgin olive oil
- Salt for pasta water
- Grated Parmesan cheese for serving

Instructions:

1. Cook the Orecchiette:

    Bring a large pot of salted water to a boil.
    Add the orecchiette pasta and cook according to the package instructions until al dente.
    Reserve 1 cup of pasta cooking water, then drain the pasta and set it aside.

2. Cook the Sausage and Broccoli Rabe:

    In a large skillet or sauté pan, cook the Italian sausage over medium heat, breaking it up with a spoon, until browned and cooked through.
    Remove the cooked sausage from the skillet and set it aside.
    In the same skillet, add the extra virgin olive oil over medium heat.
    Add the minced garlic and red pepper flakes to the skillet and cook for 1-2 minutes until fragrant.
    Add the chopped broccoli rabe to the skillet and cook, stirring occasionally, until it is wilted and tender, about 5-7 minutes.
    Return the cooked sausage to the skillet with the broccoli rabe and stir to combine. Cook for an additional 2-3 minutes to heat everything through.

3. Combine the Pasta and Sauce:

    Add the cooked orecchiette pasta to the skillet with the sausage and broccoli rabe.
    Toss everything together gently until the pasta is well coated in the sauce. If the mixture seems too dry, you can add some of the reserved pasta cooking water to loosen it up.

4. Serve:

    Transfer the Orecchiette with Broccoli Rabe and Sausage to serving plates or bowls.

Optionally, sprinkle with grated Parmesan cheese on top.
Serve immediately, piping hot, and enjoy!

Orecchiette with broccoli rabe and sausage is a hearty and satisfying dish that's perfect for a comforting meal. The combination of tender pasta, flavorful sausage, and slightly bitter broccoli rabe creates a delicious harmony of flavors.

Pappardelle with Wild Boar Ragu

Ingredients:

- 12 ounces (340g) pappardelle pasta
- 1 pound (450g) wild boar meat, ground (substitute with pork or beef if unavailable)
- 2 tablespoons olive oil
- 1 onion, finely chopped
- 2 carrots, finely chopped
- 2 celery stalks, finely chopped
- 4 cloves garlic, minced
- 1 cup red wine
- 1 can (14.5 ounces) crushed tomatoes
- 2 tablespoons tomato paste
- 1 cup beef or chicken broth
- 2 teaspoons dried oregano
- 2 teaspoons dried thyme
- Salt and freshly ground black pepper to taste
- Grated Parmesan cheese for serving
- Fresh parsley, chopped, for garnish (optional)

Instructions:

1. Prepare the Meat:

   Heat the olive oil in a large pot or Dutch oven over medium heat.
   Add the ground wild boar meat to the pot and cook, breaking it up with a spoon, until browned and cooked through.
   Remove the cooked meat from the pot and set it aside.

2. Make the Ragu Sauce:

   In the same pot, add a little more olive oil if needed.
   Add the chopped onion, carrots, and celery to the pot. Cook, stirring occasionally, until the vegetables are softened, about 5-7 minutes.
   Add the minced garlic to the pot and cook for an additional 1-2 minutes until fragrant.
   Pour in the red wine and deglaze the pot, scraping up any browned bits from the bottom.
   Add the crushed tomatoes, tomato paste, beef or chicken broth, dried oregano, and dried thyme to the pot.
   Stir in the cooked wild boar meat.

Season with salt and freshly ground black pepper to taste.

3. Simmer the Sauce:

   Bring the sauce to a simmer, then reduce the heat to low.
   Cover and let the sauce simmer gently for 1-2 hours, stirring occasionally, until thickened and flavors meld together. If the sauce becomes too thick, you can add a little more broth or water.

4. Cook the Pappardelle:

   While the sauce is simmering, bring a large pot of salted water to a boil.
   Add the pappardelle pasta and cook according to the package instructions until al dente.
   Reserve 1 cup of pasta cooking water, then drain the pasta and set it aside.

5. Combine the Pasta and Sauce:

   Add the cooked pappardelle pasta to the pot with the wild boar ragu sauce.
   Toss everything together gently until the pasta is well coated in the sauce. If the sauce seems too thick, you can add a splash of reserved pasta cooking water to loosen it up.

6. Serve:

   Transfer the Pappardelle with Wild Boar Ragu to serving plates or bowls.
   Garnish with grated Parmesan cheese and chopped fresh parsley, if desired.
   Serve immediately, piping hot, and enjoy!

Pappardelle with wild boar ragu is a hearty and satisfying dish that's perfect for a special occasion or a cozy dinner at home. The rich and flavorful sauce pairs beautifully with the wide, ribbon-like pappardelle pasta. Enjoy!

Cannelloni with Spinach and Ricotta

Ingredients:

- 12 cannelloni tubes
- 1 pound (450g) fresh spinach, washed and chopped
- 15 ounces (425g) ricotta cheese
- 1 cup grated Parmesan cheese, divided
- 2 cloves garlic, minced
- 1 egg, lightly beaten
- 1/2 teaspoon nutmeg
- Salt and freshly ground black pepper to taste
- 2 cups marinara sauce or tomato passata
- 1 cup shredded mozzarella cheese

Instructions:

1. Prepare the Cannelloni:

    Preheat your oven to 375°F (190°C).
    Cook the cannelloni tubes according to the package instructions until they are just tender. Drain and set aside.

2. Make the Filling:

    In a large mixing bowl, combine the chopped spinach, ricotta cheese, 1/2 cup grated Parmesan cheese, minced garlic, beaten egg, nutmeg, salt, and pepper. Mix until well combined.

3. Fill the Cannelloni:

    Using a small spoon or a piping bag, carefully fill each cannelloni tube with the spinach and ricotta mixture.

4. Assemble the Dish:

    Spread a thin layer of marinara sauce or tomato passata on the bottom of a baking dish.
    Arrange the filled cannelloni tubes in the baking dish in a single layer.
    Pour the remaining marinara sauce or tomato passata over the top of the cannelloni, making sure they are well coated.

Sprinkle the shredded mozzarella cheese and the remaining 1/2 cup grated Parmesan cheese over the top.

5. Bake:

    Cover the baking dish with aluminum foil and bake in the preheated oven for 25 minutes.
    Remove the foil and bake for an additional 10-15 minutes, or until the cheese is melted and bubbly and the edges are golden brown.

6. Serve:

    Once baked, remove the Cannelloni with Spinach and Ricotta from the oven.
    Let it rest for a few minutes before serving.
    Serve hot and enjoy!

Cannelloni with spinach and ricotta is a delicious and satisfying dish that's perfect for a family dinner or entertaining guests. The creamy spinach and ricotta filling pairs beautifully with the tangy marinara sauce and gooey melted cheese. Enjoy!

Bucatini all'Amatriciana

Ingredients:

- 12 ounces (340g) bucatini pasta
- 6 ounces (170g) guanciale or pancetta, diced
- 1 tablespoon olive oil
- 1 onion, finely chopped
- 2 cloves garlic, minced
- 1/2 teaspoon red pepper flakes (adjust to taste)
- 1 can (14.5 ounces) diced tomatoes
- 1/2 cup dry white wine (optional)
- Salt and freshly ground black pepper to taste
- Grated Pecorino Romano cheese for serving
- Fresh parsley, chopped, for garnish (optional)

Instructions:

1. Cook the Bucatini:

    Bring a large pot of salted water to a boil.
    Add the bucatini pasta and cook according to the package instructions until al dente.
    Reserve 1 cup of pasta cooking water, then drain the pasta and set it aside.

2. Cook the Guanciale and Onion:

    In a large skillet or sauté pan, heat the olive oil over medium heat.
    Add the diced guanciale or pancetta to the skillet and cook until it is crispy and golden brown, about 5-7 minutes.
    Add the finely chopped onion to the skillet and cook until it is softened and translucent, about 5 minutes.
    Add the minced garlic and red pepper flakes to the skillet and cook for an additional 1-2 minutes until fragrant.

3. Make the Sauce:

    If using, pour the dry white wine into the skillet and deglaze the pan, scraping up any browned bits from the bottom.
    Add the diced tomatoes to the skillet, including their juices. Stir to combine.
    Let the sauce simmer for 10-15 minutes, allowing the flavors to meld together.
    If the sauce seems too thick, you can add a splash of reserved pasta cooking water to loosen it up.

Season with salt and freshly ground black pepper to taste.

4. Combine the Pasta and Sauce:

    Add the cooked bucatini pasta to the skillet with the amatriciana sauce.
    Toss everything together gently until the pasta is well coated in the sauce.

5. Serve:

    Transfer the Bucatini all'Amatriciana to serving plates or bowls.
    Garnish with grated Pecorino Romano cheese and chopped fresh parsley, if desired.
    Serve immediately, piping hot, and enjoy!

Bucatini all'Amatriciana is a flavorful and comforting dish that celebrates the bold flavors of Italian cuisine. The combination of crispy guanciale, tangy tomatoes, and spicy red pepper flakes creates a delicious harmony of flavors. Enjoy!

Tortellini in Brodo

Ingredients:

- 8 cups (2 liters) chicken or vegetable broth
- 1 pound (450g) fresh tortellini (cheese, meat, or your preferred filling)
- Salt and freshly ground black pepper to taste
- Freshly grated Parmesan cheese for serving
- Fresh parsley, chopped, for garnish (optional)

Instructions:

1. Prepare the Broth:

   In a large pot, heat the chicken or vegetable broth over medium heat until it comes to a simmer.
   Season the broth with salt and freshly ground black pepper to taste. Adjust the seasoning according to your preference.

2. Cook the Tortellini:

   Add the fresh tortellini to the simmering broth.
   Cook the tortellini according to the package instructions or until they are al dente. This usually takes about 2-5 minutes for fresh tortellini, but refer to the package for specific cooking times.

3. Serve:

   Once the tortellini are cooked, ladle them along with the broth into serving bowls.
   Garnish each bowl with freshly grated Parmesan cheese and chopped fresh parsley, if desired.
   Serve immediately, piping hot, and enjoy!

Tortellini in Brodo is a comforting and satisfying dish, perfect for a cozy meal on a chilly day or as a starter for a special dinner. The rich and flavorful broth pairs beautifully with the tender and delicious tortellini pasta. Enjoy!

Farfalle with Pesto Genovese

Ingredients:

- 12 ounces (340g) farfalle (bowtie) pasta
- 2 cups fresh basil leaves, packed
- 1/2 cup grated Parmesan cheese
- 1/4 cup pine nuts
- 2 cloves garlic, peeled
- 1/2 cup extra virgin olive oil
- Salt and freshly ground black pepper to taste
- Grated Parmesan cheese for serving (optional)
- Fresh basil leaves for garnish (optional)

Instructions:

1. Cook the Farfalle:

   Bring a large pot of salted water to a boil.
   Add the farfalle pasta and cook according to the package instructions until al dente.
   Reserve 1 cup of pasta cooking water, then drain the pasta and set it aside.

2. Make the Pesto:

   In a food processor or blender, combine the fresh basil leaves, grated Parmesan cheese, pine nuts, and garlic cloves.
   Pulse until the ingredients are finely chopped and well combined.
   With the food processor running, slowly drizzle in the extra virgin olive oil until the pesto reaches a smooth and creamy consistency.
   Season the pesto with salt and freshly ground black pepper to taste. Adjust the seasoning according to your preference.

3. Toss the Pasta with Pesto:

   In a large mixing bowl, toss the cooked farfalle pasta with the freshly made pesto sauce until the pasta is evenly coated.
   If the pesto seems too thick, you can add a splash of reserved pasta cooking water to thin it out and help it evenly coat the pasta.

4. Serve:

   Transfer the Farfalle with Pesto Genovese to serving plates or bowls.

Optionally, sprinkle with grated Parmesan cheese and garnish with fresh basil leaves for presentation.
Serve immediately, piping hot, and enjoy!

Farfalle with Pesto Genovese is a vibrant and flavorful dish that celebrates the freshness of basil and the richness of Parmesan cheese. It's perfect for a quick and delicious meal any day of the week. Enjoy!

Cavatelli with Tomato and Basil

Ingredients:

- 12 ounces (340g) cavatelli pasta
- 4 ripe tomatoes, diced
- 4 cloves garlic, minced
- 1/4 cup extra virgin olive oil
- Salt and freshly ground black pepper to taste
- Crushed red pepper flakes (optional)
- Fresh basil leaves, torn or thinly sliced
- Grated Parmesan cheese for serving (optional)

Instructions:

1. Cook the Cavatelli:

    Bring a large pot of salted water to a boil.
    Add the cavatelli pasta and cook according to the package instructions until al dente.
    Reserve 1 cup of pasta cooking water, then drain the pasta and set it aside.

2. Prepare the Sauce:

    In a large skillet or saucepan, heat the extra virgin olive oil over medium heat.
    Add the minced garlic to the skillet and sauté for 1-2 minutes, or until fragrant.
    Add the diced tomatoes to the skillet and cook for 5-7 minutes, stirring occasionally, until they start to break down and release their juices.
    Season the tomato sauce with salt and freshly ground black pepper to taste. Add crushed red pepper flakes for a hint of heat, if desired.

3. Combine the Pasta and Sauce:

    Add the cooked cavatelli pasta to the skillet with the tomato sauce.
    Toss everything together gently until the pasta is well coated in the sauce. If the sauce seems too thick, you can add a splash of reserved pasta cooking water to loosen it up and help it adhere to the pasta.

4. Serve:

    Transfer the Cavatelli with Tomato and Basil to serving plates or bowls.
    Garnish with torn or thinly sliced fresh basil leaves.

Optionally, sprinkle with grated Parmesan cheese for extra flavor.
Serve immediately, piping hot, and enjoy!

Cavatelli with tomato and basil is a light and refreshing pasta dish that's perfect for showcasing the flavors of ripe tomatoes and fragrant basil. It's a quick and easy meal that's sure to become a favorite in your household. Buon appetito!

Paccheri with Eggplant and Mozzarella

Ingredients:

- 12 ounces (340g) paccheri pasta
- 1 large eggplant, diced
- 2 cloves garlic, minced
- 1/4 cup extra virgin olive oil, divided
- Salt and freshly ground black pepper to taste
- 1 can (14.5 ounces) diced tomatoes
- 1/2 teaspoon dried oregano
- 1/2 teaspoon dried basil
- 1/4 teaspoon crushed red pepper flakes (optional)
- 8 ounces (225g) fresh mozzarella, diced
- Fresh basil leaves, torn, for garnish
- Grated Parmesan cheese for serving (optional)

Instructions:

1. Roast the Eggplant:

    Preheat the oven to 400°F (200°C).

    Place the diced eggplant on a baking sheet lined with parchment paper.

    Drizzle with 2 tablespoons of olive oil and season with salt and pepper to taste.

    Toss the eggplant to coat evenly in the oil and seasoning.

    Roast in the preheated oven for 20-25 minutes, or until the eggplant is tender and golden brown. Set aside.

2. Cook the Paccheri:

    Bring a large pot of salted water to a boil.

    Add the paccheri pasta and cook according to the package instructions until al dente.

    Reserve 1 cup of pasta cooking water, then drain the pasta and set it aside.

3. Make the Sauce:

    In a large skillet or sauté pan, heat the remaining 2 tablespoons of olive oil over medium heat.

    Add the minced garlic to the skillet and sauté for 1-2 minutes, or until fragrant.

    Stir in the diced tomatoes, dried oregano, dried basil, and crushed red pepper flakes (if using).

Cook the sauce for 5-7 minutes, stirring occasionally, to allow the flavors to meld together.

Season the sauce with salt and pepper to taste.

4. Assemble the Dish:

    Add the roasted eggplant to the skillet with the tomato sauce.
    Toss to combine, allowing the eggplant to heat through in the sauce.
    Add the cooked paccheri pasta to the skillet and toss everything together gently until the pasta is well coated in the sauce.
    Fold in the diced fresh mozzarella until it starts to melt and become gooey.

5. Serve:

    Transfer the Paccheri with Eggplant and Mozzarella to serving plates or bowls.
    Garnish with torn fresh basil leaves and grated Parmesan cheese, if desired.
    Serve immediately, piping hot, and enjoy!

Paccheri with eggplant and mozzarella is a hearty and flavorful pasta dish that's perfect for a comforting meal any day of the week. The combination of tender pasta, roasted eggplant, gooey mozzarella, and fragrant herbs creates a truly satisfying dish. Buon appetito!

Trofie al Pesto

Ingredients:

- 12 ounces (340g) trofie pasta
- 2 cups fresh basil leaves, packed
- 1/2 cup grated Parmesan cheese
- 1/4 cup pine nuts
- 2 cloves garlic, peeled
- 1/2 cup extra virgin olive oil
- Salt, to taste
- Freshly ground black pepper, to taste
- Grated Parmesan cheese, for serving
- Optional: cherry tomatoes, halved, for garnish

Instructions:

1. Cook the Trofie Pasta:

    Bring a large pot of salted water to a boil.
    Add the trofie pasta and cook according to the package instructions until al dente.
    Reserve 1 cup of pasta cooking water, then drain the pasta and set it aside.

2. Make the Pesto Sauce:

    In a food processor or blender, combine the fresh basil leaves, grated Parmesan cheese, pine nuts, and garlic cloves.
    Pulse until the ingredients are finely chopped.
    With the food processor running, slowly drizzle in the extra virgin olive oil until the pesto reaches a smooth and creamy consistency.
    Season the pesto with salt and freshly ground black pepper to taste. Adjust the seasoning according to your preference.

3. Toss the Pasta with Pesto:

    In a large mixing bowl, toss the cooked trofie pasta with the freshly made pesto sauce until the pasta is evenly coated.
    If the pesto seems too thick, you can add a splash of reserved pasta cooking water to thin it out and help it adhere to the pasta.

4. Serve:

    Transfer the Trofie al Pesto to serving plates or bowls.

Optionally, garnish with halved cherry tomatoes and grated Parmesan cheese for extra flavor and color.
Serve immediately, piping hot, and enjoy!

Trofie al pesto is a simple yet flavorful dish that celebrates the freshness of basil and the richness of Parmesan cheese. It's perfect for a quick and delicious meal any day of the week. Enjoy!

Stuffed Shells with Ricotta and Spinach

Ingredients:

- 1 box (12 ounces) jumbo pasta shells
- 1 pound (450g) fresh spinach, chopped
- 2 cups ricotta cheese
- 1 cup grated Parmesan cheese, divided
- 2 cloves garlic, minced
- 1 egg, lightly beaten
- 1/4 teaspoon ground nutmeg
- Salt and pepper to taste
- 2 cups marinara sauce
- 1 cup shredded mozzarella cheese
- Fresh basil leaves, chopped, for garnish (optional)

Instructions:

1. Cook the Pasta Shells:

   Bring a large pot of salted water to a boil.
   Cook the jumbo pasta shells according to the package instructions until al dente.
   Drain the shells and rinse them under cold water to stop the cooking process. Set aside.

2. Prepare the Filling:

   In a large skillet, sauté the chopped spinach over medium heat until wilted and any excess moisture has evaporated. Remove from heat and let it cool.
   In a mixing bowl, combine the ricotta cheese, 1/2 cup grated Parmesan cheese, minced garlic, beaten egg, ground nutmeg, salt, and pepper.
   Once the spinach has cooled, squeeze out any excess moisture, then add it to the ricotta mixture. Stir until well combined.

3. Stuff the Shells:

   Preheat the oven to 375°F (190°C).
   Spread a thin layer of marinara sauce on the bottom of a 9x13-inch baking dish.
   Using a spoon, carefully stuff each cooked pasta shell with the ricotta and spinach mixture, and arrange them in the baking dish.

4. Bake:

   Pour the remaining marinara sauce over the stuffed shells, covering them evenly.

Sprinkle the shredded mozzarella cheese and the remaining 1/2 cup grated Parmesan cheese over the top.
Cover the baking dish with aluminum foil and bake in the preheated oven for 25 minutes.
Remove the foil and bake for an additional 10-15 minutes, or until the cheese is melted and bubbly, and the edges are golden brown.

5. Serve:

Once baked, remove the stuffed shells from the oven.
Garnish with chopped fresh basil leaves, if desired.
Serve hot and enjoy!

Stuffed shells with ricotta and spinach is a hearty and flavorful dish that's perfect for a family dinner or entertaining guests. The creamy ricotta and spinach filling pairs beautifully with the tangy marinara sauce and gooey melted cheese. Enjoy!

Spaghetti Puttanesca

Ingredients:

- 12 ounces (340g) spaghetti
- 2 tablespoons olive oil
- 4 cloves garlic, minced
- 4 anchovy fillets, finely chopped (optional)
- 1/4 teaspoon red pepper flakes (adjust to taste)
- 1 can (14.5 ounces) diced tomatoes
- 1/2 cup pitted Kalamata olives, chopped
- 2 tablespoons capers, drained
- 2 tablespoons chopped fresh parsley
- Salt and freshly ground black pepper to taste
- Grated Parmesan cheese for serving (optional)

Instructions:

1. Cook the Spaghetti:

    Bring a large pot of salted water to a boil.
    Add the spaghetti and cook according to the package instructions until al dente.
    Reserve 1 cup of pasta cooking water, then drain the spaghetti and set it aside.

2. Make the Sauce:

    In a large skillet or sauté pan, heat the olive oil over medium heat.
    Add the minced garlic, chopped anchovy fillets (if using), and red pepper flakes to the skillet. Cook for 1-2 minutes, stirring constantly, until the garlic is fragrant and the anchovies have melted into the oil.
    Add the diced tomatoes (with their juices) to the skillet. Bring to a simmer and cook for 8-10 minutes, stirring occasionally, until the sauce has thickened slightly.
    Stir in the chopped olives, capers, and chopped fresh parsley. Cook for an additional 2-3 minutes.

3. Combine the Pasta and Sauce:

    Add the cooked spaghetti to the skillet with the puttanesca sauce.
    Toss everything together gently until the spaghetti is well coated in the sauce. If the sauce seems too thick, you can add a splash of reserved pasta cooking water to loosen it up.
    Season with salt and freshly ground black pepper to taste.

4. Serve:

> Transfer the Spaghetti Puttanesca to serving plates or bowls.
> Optionally, sprinkle with grated Parmesan cheese on top.
> Serve immediately, piping hot, and enjoy!

Spaghetti Puttanesca is a flavorful and satisfying dish that's perfect for a quick and delicious weeknight dinner. The combination of briny olives, tangy capers, and savory anchovies creates a robust and irresistible sauce that pairs beautifully with spaghetti. Buon appetito!

Pappardelle with Duck Ragout

Ingredients:

For the Duck Ragout:

- 2 duck legs
- Salt and freshly ground black pepper
- 2 tablespoons olive oil
- 1 onion, finely chopped
- 2 carrots, finely chopped
- 2 celery stalks, finely chopped
- 4 cloves garlic, minced
- 1 cup dry red wine
- 1 can (14.5 ounces) diced tomatoes
- 2 cups chicken or vegetable broth
- 2 bay leaves
- 1 teaspoon dried thyme
- 1 teaspoon dried rosemary
- Salt and freshly ground black pepper to taste

For the Pappardelle:

- 12 ounces (340g) pappardelle pasta
- Salt for pasta water
- Grated Parmesan cheese for serving (optional)
- Fresh parsley, chopped, for garnish (optional)

Instructions:

1. Prepare the Duck:

    Pat the duck legs dry with paper towels and season them generously with salt and freshly ground black pepper.
    In a large Dutch oven or heavy-bottomed pot, heat the olive oil over medium-high heat. Add the duck legs to the pot, skin side down, and cook for 5-7 minutes until golden brown and crispy. Flip the duck legs and cook for an additional 5 minutes. Remove the duck legs from the pot and set them aside.

2. Make the Ragout:

In the same pot, add the chopped onion, carrots, and celery. Cook, stirring occasionally, for 5-7 minutes until the vegetables are softened.

Add the minced garlic to the pot and cook for an additional 1-2 minutes until fragrant.

Pour in the dry red wine and deglaze the pot, scraping up any browned bits from the bottom.

Stir in the diced tomatoes, chicken or vegetable broth, bay leaves, dried thyme, and dried rosemary.

Return the duck legs to the pot, nestling them into the sauce.

Bring the sauce to a simmer, then reduce the heat to low. Cover and let the ragout simmer gently for 1.5 to 2 hours, stirring occasionally, until the duck is tender and the sauce is thickened. If the sauce reduces too much, you can add a little more broth or water.

3. Cook the Pappardelle:

In a large pot of salted boiling water, cook the pappardelle pasta according to the package instructions until al dente.

Reserve 1 cup of pasta cooking water, then drain the pasta.

4. Shred the Duck and Finish the Ragout:

Once the duck is tender, remove the duck legs from the pot and shred the meat using two forks. Discard the bones and any excess fat.

Return the shredded duck meat to the pot and stir it into the ragout.

Season the ragout with additional salt and freshly ground black pepper to taste.

5. Serve:

Divide the cooked pappardelle among serving plates or bowls.

Spoon the duck ragout over the pappardelle.

Optionally, garnish with grated Parmesan cheese and chopped fresh parsley.

Serve immediately, piping hot, and enjoy!

Pappardelle with duck ragout is a hearty and comforting dish that's perfect for a special occasion or a cozy dinner at home. The tender shredded duck meat combined with the rich and flavorful sauce makes for a truly indulgent meal. Buon appetito!

Fettuccine with Shrimp Scampi

Ingredients:

- 12 ounces (340g) fettuccine pasta
- 1 pound (450g) large shrimp, peeled and deveined
- 4 tablespoons unsalted butter
- 4 cloves garlic, minced
- 1/4 teaspoon red pepper flakes (adjust to taste)
- Zest of 1 lemon
- Juice of 1 lemon
- 1/4 cup dry white wine (optional)
- Salt and freshly ground black pepper to taste
- 2 tablespoons chopped fresh parsley
- Grated Parmesan cheese for serving (optional)

Instructions:

1. Cook the Fettuccine:

    Bring a large pot of salted water to a boil.
    Add the fettuccine pasta and cook according to the package instructions until al dente.
    Reserve 1 cup of pasta cooking water, then drain the pasta and set it aside.

2. Prepare the Shrimp:

    Pat the shrimp dry with paper towels and season with salt and pepper.
    In a large skillet or sauté pan, melt 2 tablespoons of butter over medium-high heat.
    Add the shrimp to the skillet and cook for 2-3 minutes on each side, or until they are pink and opaque. Remove the shrimp from the skillet and set aside.

3. Make the Scampi Sauce:

    In the same skillet, melt the remaining 2 tablespoons of butter over medium heat.
    Add the minced garlic and red pepper flakes to the skillet. Sauté for 1-2 minutes, or until the garlic is fragrant.
    If using, pour in the dry white wine to deglaze the skillet, scraping up any browned bits from the bottom.
    Add the lemon zest and lemon juice to the skillet, stirring to combine.

Return the cooked shrimp to the skillet and toss to coat in the sauce.
Cook for an additional 1-2 minutes, allowing the flavors to meld together.
If the sauce seems too thick, you can add a splash of reserved pasta cooking water to thin it out.

4. Combine the Pasta and Sauce:

    Add the cooked fettuccine pasta to the skillet with the shrimp scampi sauce.
    Toss everything together gently until the pasta is well coated in the sauce.

5. Serve:

    Transfer the Fettuccine with Shrimp Scampi to serving plates or bowls.
    Garnish with chopped fresh parsley and grated Parmesan cheese, if desired.
    Serve immediately, piping hot, and enjoy!

Fettuccine with shrimp scampi is a quick and delicious dish that's perfect for a weeknight dinner or entertaining guests. The tender shrimp, garlic-infused butter sauce, and bright lemon flavors make this pasta dish a true crowd-pleaser. Buon appetito!

Lasagna al Forno

Ingredients:

For the Meat Sauce:

- 1 pound (450g) ground beef or Italian sausage
- 1 onion, finely chopped
- 4 cloves garlic, minced
- 1 can (14.5 ounces) crushed tomatoes
- 1 can (6 ounces) tomato paste
- 1 teaspoon dried oregano
- 1 teaspoon dried basil
- Salt and freshly ground black pepper to taste

For the Bechamel Sauce:

- 4 tablespoons unsalted butter
- 1/4 cup all-purpose flour
- 4 cups milk
- Salt and freshly ground black pepper to taste
- Pinch of ground nutmeg

Other Ingredients:

- 12 lasagna noodles, cooked according to package instructions
- 2 cups shredded mozzarella cheese
- 1 cup grated Parmesan cheese
- Fresh basil leaves, chopped, for garnish (optional)

Instructions:

1. Prepare the Meat Sauce:

   In a large skillet or saucepan, brown the ground beef or Italian sausage over medium heat, breaking it up with a spoon.
   Add the chopped onion and minced garlic to the skillet and cook until softened.
   Stir in the crushed tomatoes, tomato paste, dried oregano, dried basil, salt, and pepper.
   Simmer the sauce for about 20-30 minutes, stirring occasionally, until thickened. Adjust seasoning if needed.

2. Prepare the Bechamel Sauce:

In a medium saucepan, melt the butter over medium heat.

Whisk in the flour to create a roux and cook for 1-2 minutes until golden.

Gradually whisk in the milk, stirring constantly to avoid lumps.

Cook the sauce until thickened, about 5-7 minutes, stirring frequently.

Season with salt, pepper, and a pinch of nutmeg. Remove from heat.

3. Assemble the Lasagna:

Preheat your oven to 375°F (190°C).

Spread a thin layer of meat sauce on the bottom of a 9x13-inch baking dish.

Place a layer of cooked lasagna noodles over the sauce.

Spread a layer of meat sauce over the noodles, followed by a layer of bechamel sauce.

Sprinkle with shredded mozzarella and grated Parmesan cheese.

Repeat the layers until all ingredients are used, finishing with a layer of cheese on top.

4. Bake the Lasagna:

Cover the baking dish with aluminum foil and bake in the preheated oven for 25-30 minutes.

Remove the foil and bake for an additional 10-15 minutes, or until the cheese is melted and bubbly, and the edges are golden brown.

Let the lasagna rest for a few minutes before slicing.

Garnish with chopped fresh basil leaves, if desired, before serving.

5. Serve:

Slice the lasagna into squares and serve hot.

Enjoy your delicious homemade lasagna al forno!

Lasagna al forno is a comforting and satisfying dish that's perfect for gatherings with family and friends. The layers of pasta, savory meat sauce, creamy bechamel, and melted cheese create a decadent and irresistible meal. Buon appetito!

Linguine with Lobster

Ingredients:

- 8 ounces (225g) linguine pasta
- 2 lobster tails, cooked and meat removed from shells
- 4 tablespoons unsalted butter
- 4 cloves garlic, minced
- 1/4 cup dry white wine (optional)
- 1/2 cup seafood stock or clam juice
- Zest and juice of 1 lemon
- Salt and freshly ground black pepper to taste
- Crushed red pepper flakes (optional)
- 2 tablespoons chopped fresh parsley
- Grated Parmesan cheese for serving (optional)

Instructions:

1. Cook the Linguine:

    Bring a large pot of salted water to a boil.
    Add the linguine pasta and cook according to the package instructions until al dente.
    Reserve 1 cup of pasta cooking water, then drain the linguine and set it aside.

2. Prepare the Lobster:

    Cook the lobster tails according to your preferred method (boiling, steaming, or grilling).
    Once cooked, remove the lobster meat from the shells and chop it into bite-sized pieces.
    Set aside.

3. Make the Sauce:

    In a large skillet or sauté pan, melt the butter over medium heat.
    Add the minced garlic to the skillet and sauté for 1-2 minutes until fragrant.
    If using, pour in the dry white wine to deglaze the skillet, scraping up any browned bits from the bottom.
    Add the seafood stock or clam juice to the skillet and bring to a simmer.
    Stir in the lemon zest and juice, salt, pepper, and crushed red pepper flakes (if using).
    Let the sauce simmer for 3-4 minutes to allow the flavors to meld together.

4. Combine the Pasta and Sauce:

Add the cooked linguine pasta to the skillet with the sauce.
Toss everything together gently until the linguine is well coated in the sauce.
If the sauce seems too thick, you can add a splash of reserved pasta cooking water to thin it out.

5. Add the Lobster:

Add the chopped lobster meat to the skillet with the linguine and sauce.
Toss everything together gently to combine and heat through.

6. Serve:

Transfer the Linguine with Lobster to serving plates or bowls.
Garnish with chopped fresh parsley and grated Parmesan cheese, if desired.
Serve immediately, piping hot, and enjoy!

Linguine with lobster is a sophisticated and delicious dish that's perfect for special occasions or romantic dinners. The combination of tender lobster, garlic-infused butter sauce, and al dente linguine creates a memorable dining experience. Buon appetito!

Penne alla Vodka

Ingredients:

- 12 ounces (340g) penne pasta
- 2 tablespoons olive oil
- 4 cloves garlic, minced
- 1/4 teaspoon red pepper flakes (adjust to taste)
- 1 can (14.5 ounces) crushed tomatoes
- 1/4 cup vodka
- 1/2 cup heavy cream
- Salt and freshly ground black pepper to taste
- Fresh basil leaves, chopped, for garnish
- Grated Parmesan cheese for serving (optional)

Instructions:

1. Cook the Penne:

   Bring a large pot of salted water to a boil.
   Add the penne pasta and cook according to the package instructions until al dente.
   Reserve 1 cup of pasta cooking water, then drain the pasta and set it aside.

2. Prepare the Sauce:

   In a large skillet or saucepan, heat the olive oil over medium heat.
   Add the minced garlic and red pepper flakes to the skillet. Sauté for 1-2 minutes until fragrant.
   Pour in the crushed tomatoes and vodka. Stir to combine.
   Simmer the sauce for about 10-15 minutes, allowing the alcohol to cook off and the flavors to meld together.
   Stir in the heavy cream and continue to simmer for an additional 2-3 minutes until the sauce has thickened slightly.
   Season the sauce with salt and freshly ground black pepper to taste.

3. Combine the Pasta and Sauce:

   Add the cooked penne pasta to the skillet with the vodka sauce.
   Toss everything together gently until the penne is well coated in the sauce.
   If the sauce seems too thick, you can add a splash of reserved pasta cooking water to thin it out.

4. Serve:

    Transfer the Penne alla Vodka to serving plates or bowls.
    Garnish with chopped fresh basil leaves.
    Optionally, sprinkle with grated Parmesan cheese for extra flavor.
    Serve immediately, piping hot, and enjoy!

Penne alla vodka is a creamy and flavorful dish that's perfect for a cozy dinner at home or entertaining guests. The combination of tangy tomatoes, rich cream, and a hint of vodka creates a delicious sauce that pairs beautifully with penne pasta. Buon appetito!

Ravioli di Zucca (Pumpkin Ravioli)

Ingredients:

For the Pumpkin Filling:

- 1 cup canned pumpkin puree
- 1/2 cup ricotta cheese
- 1/4 cup grated Parmesan cheese
- 1/4 teaspoon ground nutmeg
- Salt and freshly ground black pepper to taste

For the Ravioli Dough:

- 2 cups all-purpose flour, plus extra for dusting
- 3 large eggs
- 1/2 teaspoon salt

For Serving:

- Butter or olive oil
- Sage leaves, chopped
- Grated Parmesan cheese

Instructions:

1. Make the Pumpkin Filling:

    In a mixing bowl, combine the canned pumpkin puree, ricotta cheese, grated Parmesan cheese, ground nutmeg, salt, and pepper. Mix until well combined. Adjust seasoning to taste.
    Cover the bowl with plastic wrap and refrigerate the filling while you prepare the ravioli dough.

2. Prepare the Ravioli Dough:

    On a clean work surface, mound the all-purpose flour and create a well in the center.
    Crack the eggs into the well and add the salt.
    Using a fork, gradually incorporate the flour into the eggs until a dough forms.
    Knead the dough until smooth and elastic, about 8-10 minutes.
    Wrap the dough in plastic wrap and let it rest at room temperature for at least 30 minutes.

3. Assemble the Ravioli:

    Divide the rested dough into 4 equal portions.
    Roll out each portion of dough into a thin sheet using a pasta machine or rolling pin.
    Place teaspoons of the pumpkin filling evenly spaced apart on one sheet of dough.
    Place another sheet of dough on top and press around each mound of filling to seal.
    Use a ravioli cutter or a knife to cut out individual ravioli.
    Repeat with the remaining dough and filling.

4. Cook the Ravioli:

    Bring a large pot of salted water to a boil.
    Carefully drop the ravioli into the boiling water and cook for about 3-4 minutes, or until they float to the surface.
    Remove the cooked ravioli using a slotted spoon and transfer them to a plate.

5. Serve:

    In a skillet, melt butter or heat olive oil over medium heat.
    Add the chopped sage leaves and cook until fragrant, about 1 minute.
    Toss the cooked ravioli in the sage-infused butter or olive oil.
    Serve the Pumpkin Ravioli hot, garnished with grated Parmesan cheese.

Enjoy your homemade Ravioli di Zucca with its creamy pumpkin filling and flavorful sage-infused butter! Buon appetito!

Tagliatelle with Bolognese Sauce

Ingredients:

For the Bolognese Sauce:

- 1 tablespoon olive oil
- 1 onion, finely chopped
- 2 carrots, finely chopped
- 2 celery stalks, finely chopped
- 2 cloves garlic, minced
- 1 pound (450g) ground beef or a mixture of beef and pork
- 1/4 cup tomato paste
- 1 can (14.5 ounces) crushed tomatoes
- 1 cup beef broth
- 1/2 cup red wine (optional)
- 1 teaspoon dried oregano
- 1 teaspoon dried basil
- Salt and freshly ground black pepper to taste

For the Pasta:

- 12 ounces (340g) tagliatelle pasta
- Salt for pasta water

For Serving:

- Grated Parmesan cheese
- Chopped fresh parsley

Instructions:

1. Prepare the Bolognese Sauce:

    Heat olive oil in a large skillet or Dutch oven over medium heat.
    Add chopped onion, carrots, and celery to the skillet. Cook, stirring occasionally, until vegetables are softened, about 5-7 minutes.
    Add minced garlic and cook for another minute until fragrant.
    Add ground beef to the skillet. Cook, breaking it up with a spoon, until browned and cooked through.
    Stir in tomato paste and cook for 2-3 minutes to caramelize slightly.
    Pour in crushed tomatoes, beef broth, and red wine (if using). Stir to combine.

Add dried oregano, dried basil, salt, and pepper. Bring the sauce to a simmer.
Reduce the heat to low and let the sauce simmer, uncovered, for about 1-2 hours, stirring occasionally, until it thickens and the flavors meld together. If the sauce gets too thick, you can add more beef broth or water.

2. Cook the Tagliatelle:

Bring a large pot of salted water to a boil.
Add the tagliatelle pasta to the boiling water and cook according to the package instructions until al dente.
Reserve 1 cup of pasta cooking water, then drain the pasta.

3. Combine the Pasta and Sauce:

Add the cooked tagliatelle pasta to the skillet with the Bolognese sauce.
Toss everything together gently until the pasta is well coated in the sauce. If the sauce seems too thick, you can add a splash of reserved pasta cooking water to thin it out.

4. Serve:

Transfer the Tagliatelle with Bolognese Sauce to serving plates or bowls.
Garnish with grated Parmesan cheese and chopped fresh parsley.
Serve immediately, piping hot, and enjoy!

Tagliatelle with Bolognese sauce is a comforting and satisfying meal that's perfect for a cozy dinner at home or entertaining guests. The rich and flavorful meat sauce pairs beautifully with the tender tagliatelle pasta. Buon appetito!

Orecchiette with Broccoli and Anchovies

Ingredients:

- 12 ounces (340g) orecchiette pasta
- 1 head broccoli, cut into small florets
- 4 tablespoons olive oil
- 4 cloves garlic, minced
- 4-6 anchovy fillets, chopped
- 1/4 teaspoon red pepper flakes (adjust to taste)
- Salt and freshly ground black pepper to taste
- Grated Parmesan cheese for serving (optional)
- Fresh parsley, chopped, for garnish (optional)
- Lemon zest, for garnish (optional)

Instructions:

1. Cook the Orecchiette:

    Bring a large pot of salted water to a boil.
    Add the orecchiette pasta to the boiling water and cook according to the package instructions until al dente.
    Reserve 1 cup of pasta cooking water, then drain the pasta and set it aside.

2. Blanch the Broccoli:

    While the pasta is cooking, blanch the broccoli florets in a pot of boiling salted water for about 2-3 minutes, or until tender-crisp.
    Drain the broccoli and set it aside.

3. Prepare the Sauce:

    In a large skillet or sauté pan, heat the olive oil over medium heat.
    Add the minced garlic to the skillet and sauté for 1-2 minutes until fragrant.
    Add the chopped anchovy fillets to the skillet. Cook for another 1-2 minutes, stirring, until the anchovies dissolve into the oil.
    Stir in the red pepper flakes and cook for another minute.
    Add the blanched broccoli florets to the skillet. Toss to coat in the garlic and anchovy mixture. Cook for 2-3 minutes, allowing the flavors to meld together.
    Season with salt and freshly ground black pepper to taste.

4. Combine the Pasta and Sauce:

Add the cooked orecchiette pasta to the skillet with the broccoli and anchovy mixture. Toss everything together gently until the pasta is well coated in the sauce. If the sauce seems too thick, you can add a splash of reserved pasta cooking water to thin it out.

5. Serve:

Transfer the Orecchiette with Broccoli and Anchovies to serving plates or bowls. Optionally, garnish with grated Parmesan cheese, chopped fresh parsley, and lemon zest for extra flavor.
Serve immediately, piping hot, and enjoy!

Orecchiette with broccoli and anchovies is a delicious and satisfying dish that's perfect for a quick and flavorful weeknight dinner. The combination of tender pasta, vibrant broccoli, and savory anchovies creates a delightful meal that will please your taste buds. Buon appetito!

Spaghetti alle Vongole

Ingredients:

- 12 ounces (340g) spaghetti
- 2 pounds (900g) fresh clams (such as littleneck or Manila), scrubbed and cleaned
- 4 tablespoons olive oil
- 4 cloves garlic, minced
- 1/4 teaspoon red pepper flakes (adjust to taste)
- 1/2 cup dry white wine
- Salt to taste
- Freshly ground black pepper to taste
- 1/4 cup chopped fresh parsley
- Lemon wedges, for serving (optional)
- Crushed red pepper flakes, for serving (optional)

Instructions:

1. Prepare the Clams:

    Rinse the fresh clams under cold water to remove any grit or sand.
    Discard any clams with broken shells or that do not close when tapped.
    Set the cleaned clams aside.

2. Cook the Spaghetti:

    Bring a large pot of salted water to a boil.
    Add the spaghetti to the boiling water and cook according to the package instructions until al dente.
    Reserve 1 cup of pasta cooking water, then drain the spaghetti and set it aside.

3. Cook the Clams:

    In a large skillet or sauté pan, heat the olive oil over medium heat.
    Add the minced garlic and red pepper flakes to the skillet. Sauté for 1-2 minutes until fragrant.
    Add the cleaned clams to the skillet.
    Pour in the dry white wine. Cover the skillet with a lid and cook for 5-7 minutes, or until the clams open. Discard any clams that do not open.
    Season the cooked clams with salt and freshly ground black pepper to taste.

4. Combine the Spaghetti and Clams:

> Add the cooked spaghetti to the skillet with the cooked clams and sauce.
> Toss everything together gently until the spaghetti is well coated in the sauce. If the sauce seems too dry, you can add a splash of reserved pasta cooking water to loosen it up.

5. Serve:

> Transfer the Spaghetti alle Vongole to serving plates or bowls.
> Sprinkle with chopped fresh parsley.
> Optionally, serve with lemon wedges and crushed red pepper flakes on the side for extra flavor.
> Serve immediately, piping hot, and enjoy!

Spaghetti alle Vongole is a delicious and elegant dish that's perfect for a special occasion or romantic dinner. The tender spaghetti, briny clams, and aromatic garlic and white wine sauce create a delightful flavor combination that will transport you to Italy with every bite. Buon appetito!

Tortellini alla Panna

Ingredients:

- 1 pound (450g) tortellini (cheese, meat, or your preferred filling)
- 2 tablespoons unsalted butter
- 2 cloves garlic, minced
- 1 cup heavy cream
- 1/2 cup grated Parmesan cheese
- Salt and black pepper to taste
- Fresh parsley, chopped, for garnish (optional)

Instructions:

1. Cook the Tortellini:

    Bring a large pot of salted water to a boil.
    Add the tortellini and cook according to the package instructions until al dente.
    Drain the cooked tortellini and set aside.

2. Prepare the Cream Sauce:

    In a large skillet or saucepan, melt the butter over medium heat.
    Add the minced garlic to the skillet and sauté for 1-2 minutes until fragrant.
    Pour in the heavy cream and bring to a gentle simmer.
    Let the cream simmer for a few minutes until it starts to thicken slightly.
    Stir in the grated Parmesan cheese until melted and incorporated into the sauce.
    Season with salt and black pepper to taste.

3. Combine the Tortellini and Sauce:

    Add the cooked tortellini to the skillet with the creamy sauce.
    Toss gently until the tortellini are evenly coated with the sauce.

4. Serve:

    Transfer the Tortellini alla Panna to serving plates or bowls.
    Garnish with chopped fresh parsley, if desired.
    Serve immediately, piping hot, and enjoy!

Tortellini alla Panna is a rich and comforting dish that's perfect for a cozy dinner at home. The creamy sauce complements the tender tortellini beautifully, creating a delicious and satisfying meal. Buon appetito!

Farfalle with Chicken and Sun-Dried Tomatoes

Ingredients:

- 12 ounces (340g) farfalle (bowtie) pasta
- 2 boneless, skinless chicken breasts, cut into bite-sized pieces
- Salt and pepper to taste
- 2 tablespoons olive oil
- 4 cloves garlic, minced
- 1/2 cup sun-dried tomatoes, chopped
- 1 cup chicken broth
- 1 cup heavy cream
- 1/2 cup grated Parmesan cheese
- 1 teaspoon dried Italian herbs (such as basil, oregano, and thyme)
- Fresh basil leaves, chopped, for garnish (optional)

Instructions:

1. Cook the Pasta:

    Bring a large pot of salted water to a boil.
    Add the farfalle pasta and cook according to the package instructions until al dente.
    Reserve 1 cup of pasta cooking water, then drain the pasta and set it aside.

2. Season and Cook the Chicken:

    Season the chicken pieces with salt and pepper to taste.
    Heat olive oil in a large skillet over medium-high heat.
    Add the seasoned chicken to the skillet and cook until golden brown and cooked through, about 5-6 minutes.
    Remove the cooked chicken from the skillet and set aside.

3. Make the Sauce:

    In the same skillet, add minced garlic and cook for 1-2 minutes until fragrant.
    Add chopped sun-dried tomatoes to the skillet and cook for another 2-3 minutes.
    Pour in chicken broth and bring to a simmer, scraping up any browned bits from the bottom of the skillet.
    Stir in heavy cream and simmer for 3-4 minutes until the sauce thickens slightly.
    Add grated Parmesan cheese and dried Italian herbs to the skillet. Stir until the cheese is melted and the sauce is well combined.

If the sauce seems too thick, you can add a splash of reserved pasta cooking water to thin it out.

4. Combine the Pasta, Chicken, and Sauce:

Add the cooked farfalle pasta and chicken pieces to the skillet with the sauce.
Toss everything together gently until the pasta and chicken are evenly coated with the sauce.

5. Serve:

Transfer the Farfalle with Chicken and Sun-Dried Tomatoes to serving plates or bowls.
Garnish with chopped fresh basil leaves, if desired.
Serve immediately, piping hot, and enjoy!

Farfalle with chicken and sun-dried tomatoes is a delicious and comforting meal that's perfect for a weeknight dinner or special occasion. The combination of tender pasta, flavorful chicken, and rich creamy sauce with the sweetness of sun-dried tomatoes creates a delightful taste experience. Buon appetito!

Cavatappi with Four Cheese Sauce

Ingredients:

- 12 ounces (340g) cavatappi pasta
- 2 tablespoons unsalted butter
- 2 tablespoons all-purpose flour
- 2 cups whole milk
- 1 cup shredded sharp cheddar cheese
- 1/2 cup shredded mozzarella cheese
- 1/2 cup shredded fontina cheese
- 1/2 cup shredded Gruyere cheese
- Salt and black pepper to taste
- Optional toppings: chopped parsley, breadcrumbs, or crispy bacon bits

Instructions:

1. Cook the Cavatappi:

    Bring a large pot of salted water to a boil.
    Add the cavatappi pasta and cook according to the package instructions until al dente.
    Reserve 1 cup of pasta cooking water, then drain the pasta and set it aside.

2. Make the Cheese Sauce:

    In a large saucepan, melt the butter over medium heat.
    Stir in the flour and cook, stirring constantly, for 1-2 minutes to make a roux.
    Gradually whisk in the milk until smooth.
    Cook the sauce, stirring constantly, until it thickens and coats the back of a spoon, about 5-7 minutes.
    Reduce the heat to low and gradually stir in the shredded cheeses until melted and smooth.
    Season the sauce with salt and black pepper to taste.

3. Combine the Pasta and Sauce:

    Add the cooked cavatappi pasta to the saucepan with the cheese sauce.
    Toss everything together gently until the pasta is well coated with the sauce.
    If the sauce seems too thick, you can add a splash of reserved pasta cooking water to thin it out.

4. Serve:

Transfer the Cavatappi with Four Cheese Sauce to serving plates or bowls.
If desired, sprinkle with chopped parsley, breadcrumbs, or crispy bacon bits for extra flavor and texture.
Serve immediately, piping hot, and enjoy!

Cavatappi with four cheese sauce is a decadent and comforting dish that's perfect for a cozy dinner at home. The combination of creamy cheese sauce and curly cavatappi pasta creates a delightful indulgence that will satisfy your cravings. Buon appetito!

Garganelli with Asparagus and Pancetta

Ingredients:

- 12 ounces (340g) garganelli pasta (or substitute penne or rigatoni)
- 6 ounces (170g) pancetta, diced
- 1 bunch asparagus, tough ends trimmed and cut into bite-sized pieces
- 2 cloves garlic, minced
- 1/4 cup dry white wine
- 1/2 cup heavy cream
- Salt and black pepper to taste
- Grated Parmesan cheese for serving
- Fresh parsley, chopped, for garnish

Instructions:

1. Cook the Pasta:

    Bring a large pot of salted water to a boil.
    Add the garganelli pasta and cook according to the package instructions until al dente.
    Reserve 1 cup of pasta cooking water, then drain the pasta and set it aside.

2. Cook the Pancetta and Asparagus:

    In a large skillet or sauté pan, cook the diced pancetta over medium heat until crispy and browned, about 5-7 minutes.
    Use a slotted spoon to transfer the crispy pancetta to a plate lined with paper towels to drain excess grease.
    In the same skillet with the rendered pancetta fat, add the minced garlic and cook for 1-2 minutes until fragrant.
    Add the asparagus pieces to the skillet and cook for 3-4 minutes until tender-crisp.

3. Make the Sauce:

    Deglaze the skillet with dry white wine, scraping up any browned bits from the bottom.
    Pour in the heavy cream and bring to a simmer.
    Let the cream simmer for 2-3 minutes until slightly thickened.
    Season the sauce with salt and black pepper to taste.

4. Combine the Pasta and Sauce:

> Add the cooked garganelli pasta to the skillet with the sauce.
> Toss everything together gently until the pasta is well coated with the sauce.
> If the sauce seems too thick, you can add a splash of reserved pasta cooking water to thin it out.

5. Serve:

> Transfer the Garganelli with Asparagus and Pancetta to serving plates or bowls.
> Sprinkle with the crispy pancetta pieces.
> Garnish with grated Parmesan cheese and chopped fresh parsley.
> Serve immediately, piping hot, and enjoy!

Garganelli with asparagus and pancetta is a flavorful and satisfying dish that's perfect for a special dinner or entertaining guests. The combination of tender pasta, crisp asparagus, and savory pancetta creates a delightful taste experience. Buon appetito!

Rigatoni with Eggplant and Tomato Sauce

Ingredients:

- 12 ounces (340g) rigatoni pasta
- 1 medium eggplant, diced into 1/2-inch cubes
- Salt
- 1/4 cup olive oil, divided
- 1 onion, finely chopped
- 3 cloves garlic, minced
- 1 can (14.5 ounces) diced tomatoes
- 1 can (14.5 ounces) tomato sauce
- 1 teaspoon dried oregano
- 1 teaspoon dried basil
- 1/2 teaspoon red pepper flakes (optional, for heat)
- Salt and black pepper to taste
- Grated Parmesan cheese, for serving
- Fresh basil leaves, chopped, for garnish (optional)

Instructions:

1. Cook the Rigatoni:

    Bring a large pot of salted water to a boil.
    Add the rigatoni pasta and cook according to the package instructions until al dente.
    Reserve 1 cup of pasta cooking water, then drain the pasta and set it aside.

2. Prepare the Eggplant:

    Place the diced eggplant in a colander and sprinkle generously with salt. Let it sit for about 20 minutes to draw out excess moisture and bitterness.
    After 20 minutes, rinse the eggplant thoroughly under cold water and pat dry with paper towels.

3. Sauté the Eggplant:

    In a large skillet or sauté pan, heat 2 tablespoons of olive oil over medium heat.
    Add the diced eggplant to the skillet and sauté for 8-10 minutes, or until golden brown and tender.
    Remove the cooked eggplant from the skillet and set aside.

4. Make the Tomato Sauce:

In the same skillet, add the remaining 2 tablespoons of olive oil over medium heat.
Add the chopped onion and sauté for 3-4 minutes until softened.
Add the minced garlic and sauté for another 1-2 minutes until fragrant.
Stir in the diced tomatoes, tomato sauce, dried oregano, dried basil, and red pepper flakes (if using).
Season the sauce with salt and black pepper to taste.
Let the sauce simmer for about 10-15 minutes to allow the flavors to meld together and the sauce to thicken slightly.

5. Combine the Pasta, Eggplant, and Sauce:

Add the cooked rigatoni pasta and sautéed eggplant to the skillet with the tomato sauce.
Toss everything together gently until the pasta and eggplant are well coated with the sauce.
If the sauce seems too thick, you can add a splash of reserved pasta cooking water to thin it out.

6. Serve:

Transfer the Rigatoni with Eggplant and Tomato Sauce to serving plates or bowls.
Sprinkle with grated Parmesan cheese and chopped fresh basil leaves for garnish.
Serve immediately, piping hot, and enjoy!

Rigatoni with eggplant and tomato sauce is a flavorful and comforting dish that's perfect for a satisfying dinner. The combination of tender pasta, caramelized eggplant, and rich tomato sauce creates a delicious meal that will please your taste buds. Buon appetito!

Cannelloni al Forno

Ingredients:

For the Filling:

- 1 pound (450g) ricotta cheese
- 1 cup grated Parmesan cheese
- 1 cup shredded mozzarella cheese
- 1 egg
- 1/4 cup chopped fresh parsley
- Salt and black pepper to taste

For the Sauce:

- 2 tablespoons olive oil
- 1 onion, finely chopped
- 3 cloves garlic, minced
- 1 can (14.5 ounces) crushed tomatoes
- 1 teaspoon dried basil
- 1 teaspoon dried oregano
- Salt and black pepper to taste

For Assembly:

- 12 cannelloni tubes
- 1 cup shredded mozzarella cheese
- Grated Parmesan cheese for serving
- Fresh basil leaves for garnish (optional)

Instructions:

1. Prepare the Filling:

	In a large mixing bowl, combine the ricotta cheese, grated Parmesan cheese, shredded mozzarella cheese, egg, chopped parsley, salt, and black pepper.
	Mix until well combined. Set aside.

2. Make the Sauce:

	In a saucepan, heat olive oil over medium heat.
	Add the chopped onion and garlic, and sauté until softened and fragrant, about 5 minutes.

Stir in the crushed tomatoes, dried basil, dried oregano, salt, and black pepper.
Simmer the sauce for about 15-20 minutes, stirring occasionally, until slightly thickened.
Set aside.

3. Prepare the Cannelloni:

    Preheat the oven to 375°F (190°C).
    Spread a thin layer of the tomato sauce on the bottom of a baking dish.
    Using a spoon or piping bag, fill each cannelloni tube with the ricotta cheese mixture and arrange them in a single layer in the baking dish.

4. Bake the Cannelloni:

    Pour the remaining tomato sauce over the filled cannelloni tubes, covering them evenly.
    Sprinkle shredded mozzarella cheese over the top.
    Cover the baking dish with aluminum foil and bake in the preheated oven for 25-30 minutes.
    Remove the foil and bake for an additional 10-15 minutes, or until the cheese is melted and bubbly, and the cannelloni is cooked through.

5. Serve:

    Remove the Cannelloni al Forno from the oven and let it cool slightly.
    Garnish with grated Parmesan cheese and fresh basil leaves, if desired.
    Serve hot and enjoy your delicious baked cannelloni!

Cannelloni al Forno is a comforting and satisfying dish that's perfect for a family dinner or special occasion. The combination of creamy ricotta filling, tangy tomato sauce, and gooey melted cheese makes it a crowd-pleaser every time. Buon appetito!

Fusilli with Roasted Vegetables

Ingredients:

- 12 ounces (340g) fusilli pasta
- 2 cups mixed vegetables, such as bell peppers, zucchini, cherry tomatoes, red onion, and eggplant, cut into bite-sized pieces
- 3 tablespoons olive oil
- 3 cloves garlic, minced
- 1 teaspoon dried Italian herbs (such as basil, oregano, and thyme)
- Salt and black pepper to taste
- Grated Parmesan cheese for serving
- Fresh basil leaves, chopped, for garnish (optional)

Instructions:

1. Preheat the Oven and Prepare the Vegetables:

    Preheat the oven to 400°F (200°C).
    Place the mixed vegetables on a baking sheet lined with parchment paper.
    Drizzle with 2 tablespoons of olive oil, minced garlic, dried Italian herbs, salt, and black pepper. Toss to coat the vegetables evenly.

2. Roast the Vegetables:

    Roast the vegetables in the preheated oven for 20-25 minutes, or until they are tender and slightly caramelized, stirring halfway through the cooking time.
    Once roasted, remove the vegetables from the oven and set aside.

3. Cook the Fusilli Pasta:

    While the vegetables are roasting, bring a large pot of salted water to a boil.
    Add the fusilli pasta to the boiling water and cook according to the package instructions until al dente.
    Reserve 1 cup of pasta cooking water, then drain the pasta and set it aside.

4. Combine the Pasta and Roasted Vegetables:

    In a large skillet or sauté pan, heat the remaining 1 tablespoon of olive oil over medium heat.
    Add the cooked fusilli pasta to the skillet.
    Add the roasted vegetables to the skillet with the pasta.
    Toss everything together gently until the pasta and vegetables are well combined.

If the mixture seems too dry, you can add a splash of reserved pasta cooking water to moisten it.

5. Serve:

Transfer the Fusilli with Roasted Vegetables to serving plates or bowls.
Sprinkle with grated Parmesan cheese and chopped fresh basil leaves for garnish, if desired.
Serve immediately, piping hot, and enjoy!

Fusilli with roasted vegetables is a delicious and versatile dish that's perfect for a quick and healthy weeknight dinner. The combination of tender pasta and caramelized vegetables creates a satisfying and flavorful meal that will delight your taste buds. Buon appetito!

Pappardelle with Porcini Mushrooms

Ingredients:

- 12 ounces (340g) pappardelle pasta
- 1 ounce (28g) dried porcini mushrooms
- 2 tablespoons olive oil
- 2 tablespoons unsalted butter
- 2 shallots, finely chopped
- 3 cloves garlic, minced
- 8 ounces (225g) fresh porcini mushrooms, sliced
- 1/2 cup dry white wine
- 1 cup chicken or vegetable broth
- Salt and freshly ground black pepper to taste
- 1/4 cup chopped fresh parsley
- Grated Parmesan cheese for serving

Instructions:

1. Rehydrate the Dried Porcini Mushrooms:

    Place the dried porcini mushrooms in a bowl and cover them with hot water.
    Let them soak for about 20-30 minutes, or until they are softened.
    Once softened, remove the mushrooms from the water, reserving the soaking liquid.
    Chop the rehydrated mushrooms and set them aside.

2. Cook the Pappardelle:

    Bring a large pot of salted water to a boil.
    Add the pappardelle pasta and cook according to the package instructions until al dente.
    Reserve 1 cup of pasta cooking water, then drain the pasta and set it aside.

3. Prepare the Sauce:

    In a large skillet or sauté pan, heat the olive oil and butter over medium heat.
    Add the chopped shallots and minced garlic to the skillet. Sauté for 2-3 minutes until softened and fragrant.
    Add the fresh porcini mushrooms to the skillet and cook for 5-7 minutes, or until they are golden brown and tender.
    Stir in the rehydrated chopped porcini mushrooms.
    Pour in the dry white wine and cook for 2-3 minutes until it reduces slightly.
    Add the chicken or vegetable broth and bring the mixture to a simmer.

Let the sauce simmer for 5-7 minutes until it thickens slightly. Season with salt and freshly ground black pepper to taste.

4. Combine the Pasta and Sauce:

    Add the cooked pappardelle pasta to the skillet with the porcini mushroom sauce. Toss everything together gently until the pasta is well coated with the sauce. If the sauce seems too thick, you can add a splash of reserved pasta cooking water to thin it out.

5. Serve:

    Transfer the Pappardelle with Porcini Mushrooms to serving plates or bowls.
    Sprinkle with chopped fresh parsley and grated Parmesan cheese.
    Serve immediately, piping hot, and enjoy!

Pappardelle with Porcini Mushrooms is a delightful and elegant dish that celebrates the earthy flavors of porcini mushrooms. The wide pappardelle noodles provide the perfect canvas for the rich and flavorful mushroom sauce, creating a satisfying and comforting meal. Buon appetito!

Lasagna Roll-Ups

Ingredients:

For the Lasagna Roll-Ups:

- 8 lasagna noodles
- 2 cups ricotta cheese
- 1 cup shredded mozzarella cheese
- 1/2 cup grated Parmesan cheese
- 1 egg
- 2 cloves garlic, minced
- 1/4 cup chopped fresh parsley
- Salt and pepper to taste

For the Sauce:

- 2 cups marinara sauce (store-bought or homemade)
- Additional shredded mozzarella and grated Parmesan cheese for topping

Instructions:

1. Preheat the Oven and Cook the Noodles:

    Preheat your oven to 375°F (190°C).
    Bring a large pot of salted water to a boil.
    Cook the lasagna noodles according to the package instructions until al dente.
    Drain the noodles and rinse them under cold water to stop the cooking process.
    Set them aside.

2. Prepare the Filling:

    In a mixing bowl, combine the ricotta cheese, shredded mozzarella cheese, grated Parmesan cheese, egg, minced garlic, chopped parsley, salt, and pepper. Mix until well combined.

3. Assemble the Roll-Ups:

    Lay out a cooked lasagna noodle on a clean surface.
    Spread a generous amount of the cheese mixture evenly over the entire length of the noodle.
    Carefully roll up the noodle from one end to the other, enclosing the filling inside.

Repeat with the remaining noodles and filling.

4. Add Sauce and Cheese:

    Spread a thin layer of marinara sauce on the bottom of a baking dish.
    Place the rolled-up lasagna noodles seam side down in the baking dish.
    Spoon additional marinara sauce over the top of the roll-ups.
    Sprinkle with extra shredded mozzarella and grated Parmesan cheese.

5. Bake:

    Cover the baking dish with aluminum foil and bake in the preheated oven for 20-25 minutes, or until the cheese is melted and bubbly.
    Remove the foil and continue baking for an additional 5-10 minutes, or until the cheese is golden and bubbly.

6. Serve:

    Remove the lasagna roll-ups from the oven and let them cool slightly.
    Serve the roll-ups hot, garnished with chopped parsley or basil if desired.
    Enjoy your delicious lasagna roll-ups!

Lasagna roll-ups are a crowd-pleasing dish that's perfect for a cozy family dinner or entertaining guests. You can customize the filling and sauce to your liking, making them a versatile and tasty option for any occasion. Buon appetito!

Linguine with Lemon and Garlic Shrimp

Ingredients:

- 8 ounces (225g) linguine pasta
- 1 pound (450g) large shrimp, peeled and deveined
- 4 cloves garlic, minced
- Zest of 1 lemon
- Juice of 1 lemon
- 3 tablespoons olive oil
- Salt and black pepper to taste
- Crushed red pepper flakes (optional, for heat)
- 2 tablespoons chopped fresh parsley
- Grated Parmesan cheese for serving (optional)

Instructions:

1. Cook the Linguine:

    Bring a large pot of salted water to a boil.
    Add the linguine pasta and cook according to the package instructions until al dente.
    Reserve 1 cup of pasta cooking water, then drain the pasta and set it aside.

2. Prepare the Shrimp:

    Pat the shrimp dry with paper towels and season them with salt and black pepper to taste.
    In a large skillet or sauté pan, heat 2 tablespoons of olive oil over medium-high heat.
    Add the minced garlic to the skillet and sauté for about 1 minute until fragrant.
    Add the seasoned shrimp to the skillet in a single layer and cook for 2-3 minutes per side, or until they are pink and opaque. Be careful not to overcook them.
    Once cooked, remove the shrimp from the skillet and set them aside.

3. Make the Lemon Garlic Sauce:

    In the same skillet, add the remaining 1 tablespoon of olive oil.
    Add the lemon zest and lemon juice to the skillet, stirring to combine.
    If desired, add a pinch of crushed red pepper flakes for some heat.
    Cook for 1-2 minutes, allowing the flavors to meld together.
    Adjust the seasoning with salt and black pepper to taste.

4. Combine the Linguine, Shrimp, and Sauce:

Add the cooked linguine pasta to the skillet with the lemon garlic sauce.
Toss everything together gently until the pasta is well coated with the sauce.
If the sauce seems too thick, you can add a splash of reserved pasta cooking water to thin it out.
Add the cooked shrimp back to the skillet and toss to combine.

5. Serve:

Transfer the Linguine with Lemon and Garlic Shrimp to serving plates or bowls.
Sprinkle with chopped fresh parsley and grated Parmesan cheese if desired.
Serve immediately, piping hot, and enjoy!

Linguine with lemon and garlic shrimp is a light and refreshing dish that's perfect for a quick weeknight dinner or a special occasion. The combination of tender pasta, succulent shrimp, and bright citrus flavors creates a delightful and satisfying meal. Buon appetito!

Penne with Arrabbiata Sauce

Ingredients:

- 12 ounces (340g) penne pasta
- 2 tablespoons olive oil
- 4 cloves garlic, minced
- 1/2 teaspoon red pepper flakes (adjust to taste)
- 1 can (14.5 ounces) diced tomatoes
- 1 can (6 ounces) tomato paste
- 1 teaspoon dried oregano
- 1 teaspoon dried basil
- Salt and black pepper to taste
- Fresh parsley, chopped, for garnish (optional)
- Grated Parmesan cheese for serving (optional)

Instructions:

1. Cook the Penne:

    Bring a large pot of salted water to a boil.
    Add the penne pasta and cook according to the package instructions until al dente.
    Reserve 1 cup of pasta cooking water, then drain the pasta and set it aside.

2. Prepare the Arrabbiata Sauce:

    In a large skillet or saucepan, heat the olive oil over medium heat.
    Add the minced garlic and red pepper flakes to the skillet. Sauté for 1-2 minutes until the garlic is fragrant and the red pepper flakes are toasted.
    Stir in the diced tomatoes (with their juices) and tomato paste.
    Add the dried oregano and dried basil to the skillet. Season with salt and black pepper to taste.
    Bring the sauce to a simmer and let it cook for 10-15 minutes, stirring occasionally, until it thickens slightly.

3. Combine the Penne and Sauce:

    Add the cooked penne pasta to the skillet with the arrabbiata sauce.
    Toss everything together gently until the pasta is well coated with the sauce. If the sauce seems too thick, you can add a splash of reserved pasta cooking water to thin it out.

4. Serve:

Transfer the Penne with Arrabbiata Sauce to serving plates or bowls.
Garnish with chopped fresh parsley and grated Parmesan cheese if desired.
Serve immediately, piping hot, and enjoy!

Penne with Arrabbiata Sauce is a spicy and flavorful dish that's perfect for pasta lovers who enjoy a bit of heat. The combination of tangy tomatoes, aromatic garlic, and fiery red pepper flakes creates a satisfying and comforting meal. Buon appetito!

Ravioli with Spinach and Ricotta

Ingredients:

- 1 package of fresh or frozen ravioli (about 20-24 pieces)
- 2 cups fresh spinach leaves, chopped
- 1 cup ricotta cheese
- 1/2 cup grated Parmesan cheese
- 2 cloves garlic, minced
- 1 egg, lightly beaten
- Salt and pepper to taste
- 2 tablespoons olive oil
- Optional: Marinara sauce or Alfredo sauce for serving
- Grated Parmesan cheese and chopped fresh parsley for garnish

Instructions:

1. Cook the Ravioli:

    Bring a large pot of salted water to a boil.
    Add the ravioli to the boiling water and cook according to the package instructions if using fresh ravioli, or for a few minutes longer if using frozen ravioli, until they float to the surface and are cooked through.
    Once cooked, remove the ravioli from the water using a slotted spoon and set them aside. Reserve about 1/2 cup of the pasta cooking water.

2. Prepare the Filling:

    In a large mixing bowl, combine the chopped spinach, ricotta cheese, grated Parmesan cheese, minced garlic, beaten egg, salt, and pepper. Mix until well combined.

3. Fill the Ravioli:

    Lay out the cooked ravioli on a clean work surface.
    Spoon a small amount of the spinach and ricotta mixture onto each ravioli.
    Fold the ravioli over the filling to create a half-moon shape, pressing the edges to seal.

4. Cook the Ravioli:

    In a large skillet, heat the olive oil over medium heat.

Place the filled ravioli in the skillet in a single layer, being careful not to overcrowd the pan.
Cook the ravioli for 2-3 minutes per side, or until they are lightly golden and crispy.

5. Serve:

Transfer the cooked ravioli to serving plates or bowls.
Serve with your choice of marinara sauce or Alfredo sauce drizzled over the top.
Garnish with grated Parmesan cheese and chopped fresh parsley.
Serve immediately and enjoy!

Ravioli with spinach and ricotta is a delicious and satisfying dish that's perfect for a cozy dinner at home. The creamy filling pairs perfectly with the tender pasta, creating a comforting and flavorful meal. Buon appetito!

Spaghetti alla Puttanesca

Ingredients:

- 12 ounces (340g) spaghetti
- 2 tablespoons olive oil
- 4 cloves garlic, minced
- 4 anchovy fillets, chopped (optional)
- 1 can (14.5 ounces) diced tomatoes
- 1/2 cup pitted Kalamata olives, chopped
- 2 tablespoons capers, drained
- 1/4 teaspoon red pepper flakes (adjust to taste)
- Salt and black pepper to taste
- Chopped fresh parsley for garnish
- Grated Parmesan cheese for serving (optional)

Instructions:

1. Cook the Spaghetti:

    Bring a large pot of salted water to a boil.
    Add the spaghetti and cook according to the package instructions until al dente.
    Reserve 1 cup of pasta cooking water, then drain the spaghetti and set it aside.

2. Prepare the Sauce:

    In a large skillet or sauté pan, heat the olive oil over medium heat.
    Add the minced garlic and chopped anchovy fillets (if using) to the skillet. Sauté for 1-2 minutes until the garlic is fragrant and the anchovies have melted into the oil.
    Stir in the diced tomatoes (with their juices), chopped olives, capers, and red pepper flakes.
    Season the sauce with salt and black pepper to taste.
    Let the sauce simmer for about 10-15 minutes, stirring occasionally, until it thickens slightly.

3. Combine the Spaghetti and Sauce:

    Add the cooked spaghetti to the skillet with the puttanesca sauce.
    Toss everything together gently until the spaghetti is well coated with the sauce. If the sauce seems too thick, you can add a splash of reserved pasta cooking water to thin it out.

4. Serve:

> Transfer the Spaghetti alla Puttanesca to serving plates or bowls.
> Garnish with chopped fresh parsley.
> Serve immediately, piping hot, and enjoy!

Spaghetti alla Puttanesca is a bold and flavorful dish that's perfect for lovers of Mediterranean cuisine. The combination of briny olives, tangy capers, and aromatic garlic creates a vibrant sauce that pairs perfectly with the tender spaghetti. Serve it with a sprinkle of grated Parmesan cheese on top if desired. Buon appetito!

Tagliatelle with Creamy Mushroom Sauce

Ingredients:

- 300g tagliatelle pasta
- 300g mushrooms (such as button mushrooms or cremini), sliced
- 2 tablespoons olive oil
- 2 cloves garlic, minced
- 1 small onion, finely chopped
- 1 cup heavy cream
- 1/2 cup grated Parmesan cheese
- Salt and pepper to taste
- Fresh parsley, chopped (for garnish)

Instructions:

Cook the Tagliatelle:
- Bring a large pot of salted water to a boil.
- Add the tagliatelle pasta and cook according to the package instructions until al dente.
- Once cooked, drain the pasta and set aside, reserving about 1/2 cup of the pasta water.

Prepare the Mushroom Sauce:
- Heat the olive oil in a large skillet over medium heat.
- Add the minced garlic and chopped onion to the skillet and sauté until fragrant and softened, about 2-3 minutes.
- Add the sliced mushrooms to the skillet and cook until they release their moisture and become tender, about 5-7 minutes.
- Pour in the heavy cream and stir to combine with the mushrooms, garlic, and onion.
- Let the sauce simmer gently for a few minutes until it thickens slightly.
- Stir in the grated Parmesan cheese until melted and well combined.
- If the sauce seems too thick, you can add some of the reserved pasta water to thin it out to your desired consistency.
- Season the sauce with salt and pepper to taste.

Combine Pasta and Sauce:
- Add the cooked tagliatelle pasta to the skillet with the mushroom sauce.
- Toss the pasta gently in the sauce until it is well coated.
- Cook for an additional minute or two, allowing the pasta to absorb some of the flavors of the sauce.

Serve:
- Once the pasta is heated through and coated evenly with the sauce, remove the skillet from the heat.
- Transfer the tagliatelle with creamy mushroom sauce to serving plates or a large serving dish.
- Garnish with chopped fresh parsley for a pop of color and added flavor.
- Serve hot and enjoy!

This creamy mushroom sauce pairs beautifully with the delicate texture of tagliatelle pasta, making it a perfect dish for a cozy dinner at home or a special occasion. Feel free to customize the recipe by adding other herbs or vegetables according to your taste preferences. Buon appetito!

Orecchiette with Sausage and Broccoli Rabe

Ingredients:

- 350g orecchiette pasta
- 300g Italian sausage (sweet or spicy), casings removed
- 1 bunch broccoli rabe, washed and trimmed
- 3 cloves garlic, minced
- 1/4 cup extra virgin olive oil
- Salt and black pepper to taste
- Crushed red pepper flakes (optional)
- Grated Parmesan cheese for serving

Instructions:

Prepare the Broccoli Rabe:
- Bring a large pot of salted water to a boil.
- Blanch the broccoli rabe in the boiling water for 2-3 minutes, or until it's just tender.
- Remove the broccoli rabe from the pot using tongs or a slotted spoon and immediately transfer it to a bowl of ice water to stop the cooking process.
- Once cooled, drain the broccoli rabe and chop it into bite-sized pieces. Set aside.

Cook the Orecchiette:
- In the same pot of boiling water used for the broccoli rabe, cook the orecchiette pasta according to the package instructions until al dente.
- Before draining the pasta, reserve about 1 cup of the pasta cooking water. Then drain the pasta and set it aside.

Cook the Sausage and Garlic:
- While the pasta is cooking, heat the olive oil in a large skillet over medium heat.
- Add the minced garlic to the skillet and sauté for about 1 minute, until fragrant.
- Crumble the Italian sausage into the skillet and cook, breaking it apart with a spoon, until it's browned and cooked through.

Combine Ingredients:
- Once the sausage is cooked, add the chopped broccoli rabe to the skillet.
- Stir everything together and cook for an additional 2-3 minutes to allow the flavors to meld.
- If desired, season with salt, black pepper, and crushed red pepper flakes to taste.

Bring It All Together:
- Add the cooked orecchiette pasta to the skillet with the sausage and broccoli rabe.
- Toss everything together gently, adding some of the reserved pasta cooking water if needed to loosen the sauce and help it coat the pasta evenly.
- Cook for another minute or two until everything is heated through and well combined.

Serve:
- Divide the orecchiette with sausage and broccoli rabe among serving plates.
- Sprinkle with grated Parmesan cheese on top.

- Serve hot, and enjoy your delicious meal!

This dish is full of hearty flavors and textures, making it perfect for a satisfying weeknight dinner or a special occasion. Feel free to adjust the seasoning and spice levels to suit your taste preferences. Buon appetito!

Farfalle with Salmon and Cream Sauce

Ingredients:

- 350g farfalle pasta
- 300g salmon fillet, skin removed
- Salt and black pepper to taste
- 2 tablespoons olive oil
- 2 cloves garlic, minced
- 1 small onion, finely chopped
- 1 cup heavy cream
- 1/2 cup grated Parmesan cheese
- 1 tablespoon lemon juice
- 2 tablespoons fresh dill, chopped (or 1 teaspoon dried dill)
- 1 tablespoon capers, drained (optional)
- Lemon zest for garnish (optional)

Instructions:

Cook the Farfalle:
- Bring a large pot of salted water to a boil.
- Add the farfalle pasta and cook according to the package instructions until al dente.
- Once cooked, drain the pasta and set aside.

Prepare the Salmon:
- Season the salmon fillet with salt and black pepper on both sides.
- Heat 1 tablespoon of olive oil in a skillet over medium-high heat.
- Place the salmon fillet in the skillet, skin-side down, and cook for 3-4 minutes until the skin is crispy.
- Flip the salmon and cook for another 2-3 minutes until it's cooked through and flakes easily with a fork.
- Remove the salmon from the skillet and flake it into bite-sized pieces using a fork. Set aside.

Make the Cream Sauce:
- In the same skillet used for the salmon, add the remaining tablespoon of olive oil.
- Add the minced garlic and chopped onion to the skillet and sauté until softened and fragrant, about 2-3 minutes.
- Pour in the heavy cream and bring it to a gentle simmer.

- Stir in the grated Parmesan cheese until it's melted and the sauce is smooth.
- Add the lemon juice, chopped dill, and capers (if using) to the sauce.
- Season the sauce with salt and black pepper to taste.

Combine Pasta, Salmon, and Sauce:
- Add the cooked farfalle pasta to the skillet with the cream sauce.
- Toss gently to coat the pasta evenly with the sauce.
- Add the flaked salmon pieces to the skillet and toss again gently to combine, being careful not to break up the salmon too much.

Serve:
- Divide the farfalle with salmon and cream sauce among serving plates.
- Garnish with lemon zest and additional chopped dill, if desired.
- Serve hot and enjoy your delicious meal!

This farfalle with salmon and cream sauce is a perfect balance of flavors and textures, making it a great choice for a special dinner or entertaining guests. Adjust the seasoning and garnishes according to your taste preferences, and enjoy!

Cavatelli with Rapini and Sausage

Ingredients:

- 350g cavatelli pasta
- 300g Italian sausage (sweet or spicy), casings removed
- 1 bunch rapini (also known as broccoli rabe), washed and trimmed
- 3 cloves garlic, minced
- 1/4 cup extra virgin olive oil
- Salt and black pepper to taste
- Grated Parmesan cheese for serving

Instructions:

Prepare the Rapini:
- Bring a large pot of salted water to a boil.
- Blanch the rapini in the boiling water for about 2-3 minutes, or until it's just tender.
- Remove the rapini from the pot using tongs or a slotted spoon and immediately transfer it to a bowl of ice water to stop the cooking process.
- Once cooled, drain the rapini and chop it into bite-sized pieces. Set aside.

Cook the Cavatelli:
- In the same pot of boiling water used for the rapini, cook the cavatelli pasta according to the package instructions until al dente.
- Before draining the pasta, reserve about 1 cup of the pasta cooking water. Then drain the pasta and set it aside.

Cook the Sausage and Garlic:
- While the pasta is cooking, heat the olive oil in a large skillet over medium heat.
- Add the minced garlic to the skillet and sauté for about 1 minute, until fragrant.
- Crumble the Italian sausage into the skillet and cook, breaking it apart with a spoon, until it's browned and cooked through.

Combine Ingredients:
- Once the sausage is cooked, add the chopped rapini to the skillet.
- Stir everything together and cook for an additional 2-3 minutes to allow the flavors to meld.
- If desired, season with salt and black pepper to taste.

Bring It All Together:
- Add the cooked cavatelli pasta to the skillet with the sausage and rapini.

- Toss everything together gently, adding some of the reserved pasta cooking water if needed to loosen the sauce and help it coat the pasta evenly.
- Cook for another minute or two until everything is heated through and well combined.

Serve:
- Divide the cavatelli with rapini and sausage among serving plates.
- Sprinkle with grated Parmesan cheese on top.
- Serve hot, and enjoy your delicious meal!

This dish is full of robust flavors and textures, making it perfect for a satisfying weeknight dinner or a special occasion. Adjust the seasoning and spice levels to suit your taste preferences. Buon appetito!

Rigatoni with Cherry Tomato Sauce and Burrata

Ingredients:

- 350g rigatoni pasta
- 500g cherry tomatoes, halved
- 2 cloves garlic, minced
- 2 tablespoons extra virgin olive oil
- Salt and black pepper to taste
- 1/4 teaspoon red pepper flakes (optional)
- 1 ball of burrata cheese
- Fresh basil leaves, torn, for garnish
- Grated Parmesan cheese, for serving (optional)

Instructions:

Prepare the Cherry Tomato Sauce:
- In a large skillet, heat the olive oil over medium heat.
- Add the minced garlic and cook for about 1 minute, until fragrant.
- Add the halved cherry tomatoes to the skillet.
- Season with salt, black pepper, and red pepper flakes (if using).
- Cook the tomatoes for about 10-15 minutes, stirring occasionally, until they start to soften and break down, and the sauce thickens slightly.
- Use a fork or the back of a spoon to crush some of the tomatoes to release their juices.

Cook the Rigatoni:
- While the cherry tomato sauce is simmering, bring a large pot of salted water to a boil.
- Add the rigatoni pasta to the boiling water and cook according to the package instructions until al dente.
- Once cooked, drain the pasta, reserving about 1/2 cup of the pasta cooking water.

Combine Pasta and Sauce:
- Add the cooked rigatoni pasta to the skillet with the cherry tomato sauce.
- Toss the pasta gently to coat it evenly with the sauce.
- If the sauce seems too thick, you can add some of the reserved pasta cooking water to loosen it up.

Serve:
- Transfer the rigatoni with cherry tomato sauce to serving plates or a large serving dish.

- Tear the burrata cheese into chunks and place them on top of the pasta.
- Garnish with torn fresh basil leaves.
- Optionally, sprinkle with grated Parmesan cheese for an extra burst of flavor.
- Serve immediately, allowing the warmth of the pasta to melt the creamy burrata cheese into the sauce.

Enjoy!

This dish is best served immediately while the burrata is still creamy and the pasta is hot. It's perfect for a cozy dinner at home or for entertaining guests. Enjoy the burst of flavors from the sweet cherry tomatoes and the creamy richness of the burrata cheese!

www.ingramcontent.com/pod-product-compliance
Lightning Source LLC
LaVergne TN
LVHW061940070526
838199LV00060B/3896